The God in Every Body Book

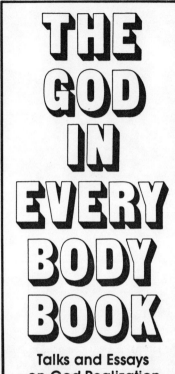

THE GOD IN EVERY BODY BOOK

Talks and Essays on God-Realization

DA FREE JOHN

Edited by Saniel Bonder and Georg Feuerstein

THE DAWN HORSE PRESS
CLEARLAKE, CALIFORNIA

First edition February 1983
Second edition October 1983

Printed in the United States of America
International Standard Book Number
paper 0-913922-78-1

Produced by The Johannine Daist Communion
in cooperation with The Dawn Horse Press

Contents

Introduction

If there is a single word that characterizes our present-day civilization, it is *doubt*. For, our whole way of life and thinking about the world and about ourselves is influenced, even governed, by the ideology of scientism. And scientism is based on the scientific method of doubt, blown out of all proportions: It calls everything into question, particularly whatever cannot be reduced to visible, or at least measurable, "hard facts." Its ruling maxim is "Seeing is believing."

Scientism is the "religion" of scientific materialism. Ever since the advent of the "new" scientific spirit in the seventeenth century, scientists have been at loggerheads with the Church and religion in general. As scientism grew in power and influence, it became increasingly hostile toward, and more openly critical of, religion and metaphysics. Theology, which had been "the Queen of Sciences" throughout the Middle Ages, was swiftly dethroned. Then, toward the end of the nineteenth century, Nietzsche boldly proclaimed the "death" of God. Man himself was deified. Mankind had ceased to marvel at, and be awe-inspired by, the mystery of the universe, within and without. Instead, scientists and then also laymen began to put their faith in the progress of science, which one day would provide a rational answer to all Man's questions.

True, science has answered a great many questions. But it has also raised a good many new ones. The original hope of unlimited progress has been shattered. Instead of leading humanity into a Golden Age of Plenty, science and technology have given rise to all kinds of social problems and perils that today threaten the human race with extinction.

The world's religions have failed to provide an antidote to the poison of scientific materialism. It has succeeded in paralyzing the minds and numbing the hearts of the majority of men and women alive today. Most people nowadays, if they are not self-declared atheists or agnostics, have no more than a lukewarm interest in spiritual life. How many merely pay lip service to the religion of their birth? How many are either apologetic about their belief in God or ostentatious about it because it profits them? There are very few people who do not merely believe in the existence of God, but actually live on the basis of heartfelt faith or intuition of the Divine.

Having ousted religion, scientific materialism has failed to bring mankind equanimity, contentment, fulfillment, or happiness. There is a widespread discontent and disillusionment in life, which drives some to a restless search for ever-new experiences and adventures, others to the couches of psychoanalysts or to mental asylums, and yet others to quiet despair, alcoholism, or suicide. In the last analysis, Man's present disorientation and experience of meaninglessness are a direct result of his having been torn out of the protective environment of traditional religion. So long as there was only one belief system, one Church, each man "knew" his place in the universe. He was not confused by competing values and beliefs. He may, at times, have querulously argued with his Creator for what he felt was an unjust lot. But he would never have doubted God's existence. Then, when he was taught that God was fashioned in Man's own image (rather than Man in the image of God), he lost his childlike, naive faith. Thus, humanity was forced out of its childhood, facing the challenge of growing into maturity.

Although scientism would have us believe that Man has at last come of age, the truth is that for the most part he has barely passed through the rebellious years of adolescence. In its origins and orientation, scientism itself is a form of adolescent protest, combined with Man's search for an identity in the face of the global changes initiated by science and technology. Where people do not simply fall back into a disposition of childish dependency, in the form of religious provincialism, they espouse an adolescent, skeptical point of view. Few bypass these two pseudo-solutions. In other words, many people either revert to blind faith, to the unexamined belief in a paternalistic Creator-Deity, or they adopt (equally blindly) the positivistic *belief* that God is an unprovable and hence nonexistent entity. According to this view, God is merely a meaningless concept, a phantasm of human language.

And yet, belief in God and talk about God has proven extraordinarily resilient, despite the onslaught of materialist philosophy over two centuries. Indeed, religion is at present experiencing a remarkable comeback. Christianity, Islam, Hinduism, and Buddhism as well as other minor traditions find themselves in the middle of a renaissance. However, this religious revival is in many cases only a regeneration of the "heresy" of religious provincialism, that is, the dogmatism of religious half-truths—sectarian and cultic fanaticism.

What has happened to authentic religion or spirituality? What has happened to the *Realization* of the Living God— the great Testimony of the Adepts? What is current today is merely the abstract idea of "God," or the belief in a parental "God" who hears one's prayers, or the drug-induced experience of "God." But these encounters with "God" are all products of the striving ego. They are encounters with the "God" whose death was declared a century ago.

The Living God, however, cannot be thought, emoted, or experienced. The Divine Reality cannot be affirmed or denied. It can only be Realized. This is the great truth that has been kept alive in the high esoteric traditions. It has never been a part of exoteric or popular religion, which demands adherence rather than genuine self-sacrifice. For, to Realize the Living God presupposes utter self-transcendence, perfect surrender of the ego. This is the glorious Teaching of all the God-Realized Adepts of mankind. It is also the Evangel of Master Da Free John. His whole life of self-transcending surrender is a Demonstration of the Truth that the God beyond all thought and experience is *not* dead. In the words of the Adept Da Free John:

> God is the Truth of Nature, not merely the Creator of Nature. This is affirmed by all the great Adepts, and I likewise affirm it on the basis of Realization, not hearsay.[1]
>
> There is no higher world to which we should aspire. Our aspiration should be toward the Present God, toward a state of perfect Identification with the Living God. This disposition does not aspire toward transitions to other worlds or a temporary transition out of this world and a return to it. The perfect fulfillment of this Way is demonstrated through Translation, or the complete dissolution of the habit-energies of attention that lead toward conditional embodiment and experiencing. It is not by aspiring to go elsewhere that we enter into the Divine Domain but by entering directly into the Living Divine, always, presently.[2]

This slim volume presents a selection of Master Da Free John's talks and essays in which he speaks of modern Man's failure to move beyond mere doubt, complacency, and conventional religiosity, and of Man's prior Enlightenment or Happiness. Master Da has been considering these matters of

---

1. Da Free John, *The Fire Gospel: Essays and Talks on Spiritual Baptism* (The Dawn Horse Press, 1982), p. 49.

2. Ibid., p. 88.

the great Way of Truth with devotees for many years, always finding new ways of expressing the Obvious. These talks and essays are by no means mere intellectual exercises generated for the edification or mental stimulation of others. Rather, their sole purpose is to Awaken others to the direct Intuition of the Divine Reality.

If God is indeed Alive, what will you do?

The Editors

PART I

Does God Exist?

Introduction to Part I

Throughout this book Master Da Free John speaks of
God in positive terms as Truth, Reality, Spirit, Consciousness, the "Radiant Transcendental Being." He thus
stands in the great Tradition of Adepts or Divine Teachers
such as Jesus and Krishna who have Realized and ecstatically
praised and pointed to the Living Absolute Reality, Transcendental Person, and Happiness that is God. But the Way that
Master Da offers does not in any way require or revolve
around an idealistic *belief* in God in any form. Rather, Master
Da only calls people to listen to his "Teaching Argument"
and, on its basis, to observe and freely consider their own
actual, present situation and existence. In this regard, Master
Da's Way is similar to the "realistic" approach offered by
Gautama the Buddha, which is based upon direct examination
of the nature of one's present existence, without resort to any
metaphysical beliefs.

In the Way that Master Da Teaches, faith in God or the
Divine Reality is awakened as a matter of heartfelt intuitive
realization or certainty, rather than mere belief or logical
assumption. This process was first demonstrated in Master
Da's own life. Though born Illumined, he had to pass through
the apparent loss and arduous recovery of the state of Divine
Realization. Through that passage he became uniquely
sensitive to the modern spiritual crisis and the Way whereby
others may Realize God just as he has. He once spoke of these
matters to devotees:

> If there is a God, then, viewing this world, why
> should one become the devotee of such a One? It would
> seem more appropriate to give such a God short shrift!
> (Laughter.) And basically that is what everybody does.

Everybody is born, goes through a difficult childhood or time of learning, and then is expected to manage his life more or less on his own. And then, on the basis of experience and all the News that comes along every day, he or she makes a judgment about how to relate to manifest existence. That judgment is not really a decision. It is the product of a whole life of reactions or rituals built up over time, a mediocre life that is basically not oriented to anything subtler than the solid world that appears by our ordinary experience. It is essentially a mortal affair, unillumined, moving by tendency and the rituals of life in common with others toward death—a death in bed, hopefully! (Laughter.)

Then, along with all of that, everybody has the question, "Is there a God?" Everybody deals with this question in one way or another. And some say, "Yes."

I have never been convinced by anybody who said he or she believed in God. I have never believed a single person who has told me that. You can feel in such people the kind of sulking disbelief that is not even quite so evident in an atheist. (Laughter.) Generally they have made this so-called "decision" for belief because they were brought up in a very strong religious background by strong parents, and they were weak, emotional, and impressionable. In any case such a decision is based on experience, on reaction to the quality of life.

Those who say they believe in God really mean that they think that they have not created the world—which is a very intelligent assumption! Since they have not created the world, Something Else is responsible for it. So we get the idea of God as Creator, or Creative, and then all the other adjectives that get added after that one, and thus we get the naive, traditional religious point of view.

In the course of my own spiritual re-Awakening I passed through many kinds of experiences, mystical visions and transports, yogic transformations, and transcendental intuitive realizations. But all of that became only instruction for me, only a lesson, because it became clear that none of what I had been shown was itself God or Truth. At last there was perfect dissolution in God. And in that Divine Realization God is no longer conceived, God is no longer measured on the basis of experience. God is no longer known as the Creator. No judgment is made. That Realization is not a matter of embracing or of excluding the world. Neither is it a matter of embracing God. In that Realization all things obviously appear in the Divine, but God is no longer analyzed out and separated from the world and from individual consciousness by that logic. Thus, all of the logical realizations that precede the moment of God-Realization are undone in the paradox of the Realization of God in Truth.

January 11, 1976

Just as he himself did not proceed on the basis of either belief or disbelief in God, but by relying on passionate, concentrated "listening" or direct examination of all his experience, so Master Da invites all others simply to examine their experience, freely and directly, on the basis of his critical Argument. Such "listening" is the necessary beginning and constant foundation of practice of the Way that he Teaches. At the outset it does not involve prayer, nor what we commonly call meditation. It only involves "combining" ourselves with his Argument through intense attention, feeling, and self-inspection.

Part One of this book presents Master Da's Teaching Argument relative to the nature and existence of "the God in

Every Body" (the self of all beings and the Source-Condition of all phenomena) and the roots of both doubt and true faith in Man.

The Editors

The Parental Deity and the One to Be Realized

a talk by Da Free John

MASTER DA: I was speaking earlier today with a couple of devotees about the notion that people have of God. I was talking to them about their childhood upbringing and the religious ideas of their childhood. There is a common notion people have that they associate with God or the Divine and which they commonly identify as a basic religious feeling or concept. I described it as a feeling you may have that, even when you are alone, there is Somebody Else in the room. I was pointing out to them that this is just the opposite or the antithesis of the point of view of real spiritual life. I am speaking about God all the time, but actually I am making a different proposition or speaking from a point of view that is different from the conventional religious one. Perhaps, by contrast, we could say that this point of view I am considering with you is summarized in the notion that, no matter how many people are in the room, there is still only One Person there! (Laughter.)

In general, discussions about God or religion tend to be associated naively with this idea of the "Other" Power, the "Other" One. This idea corresponds to a rather childish or infantile sense of Reality. Children, you see, are not in general great metaphysicians or great mystics! They have some very primitive kinds of awareness, as well as some remarkable kinds of awareness that adults tend to lose or dismiss. But when they communicate about their feeling of God, they very often express a feeling that has been dictated to them by their parents. They naively describe Reality according to a child's psychology, that free, child-made awareness of total Reality which is not natively associated with great, abstract propositions. It is not that children are free of mind, and therefore their religious concepts are purer than those of adults. The religious concepts to which a child can be sensitive and responsive are generally built upon the psychology of his or her situation, which is one of being dependent on a parent or parents, particularly on the mother. The parent-child relationship, in which the parent is a great, experienced person there to protect the smaller, vulnerable person, provides the naive basis for childish religious views and for what we commonly call religious views in general. In other words, the notion that we have of God, prior to or apart from God-Realization itself, tends to be a carry-over, an extension of our childish situation. Religion tends therefore to be a solution for a rather infantile problem: the need to be protected, sustained, and made to feel that everything is all right and that everything is going to be all right, the need to feel that there is a superior, Other Power that is in charge of everything.

When people commonly communicate to their children about God, they speak of God as a kind of super-version of mommy and daddy. When we speak to one another about our earliest religious consciousness (and it is more a kind of consciousness or mental attitude than it is an experience), we commonly talk to one another in the terms of a child's model of Reality. In fact, to enter truly into the religious process you must transcend the child's version of Reality. To become human, to be an adult, a mature human personality, you should have overcome that childish view, but commonly people do not. Thus, to the degree that people are religious, it is that portion of themselves that is basically childish or infantile that is being religious or that needs religion. The whole domain of religion is commonly the domain of subhumanity, or of childishness and adolescence rather than real human maturity. When we believe in God, what we are actually believing is that everything that is outside of ourselves is ultimately epitomized in some Person, Force, or Being that is not merely making and controlling everything, but is in charge and is going to protect us. And, especially, that this Other Person will protect us and even help us to get a lot of things we want if we will enter into a special kind of relationship with that One. That relationship is very similar to the one that we were called to enter into with our parents: "Be good and we will love you and protect you and give you things that you want."

Thus, popular religion is largely a cultural domain of social morality. People are asked to behave in one or another fashion that we would call "good" in order to maintain a good association with the parentlike God, so that they will be loved and protected by that One and given the things they want while they are alive and after death.

Religion is therefore largely an enterprise of our childhood, of our dependent, childish state. When people become adults, however, they have more hard facts to deal with in life. They feel much less protected than they did as children in the household of their parents. So they begin to question and to doubt the existence of this Parental Deity. Such individuals may continue to be religious in some sense, willing to play the game of social morality and good behavior, but they carry on a rather adolescent relationship of dependence-independence, or embrace and withdrawal, relative to this God-Person.

Atheism is the ultimate form of denial of the Parental God. It is not founded on real experiences of the ultimate facts of the universe. It is itself a kind of adolescent development of the human species. What characterizes the doctrine or dogma of atheism is not a discovery that there is no God, but a refusal to acknowledge the Parental God of childish religion.

If such religion amounts to an experience rather than just a kind of consciousness or a state of mind, it could basically be defined as a very primitive sense that invades all of your life, but that relates to you most specifically in your solitariness, your individuality. It is the sense that when you are alone (and you are in some sense always alone, in that you have a private destiny), Somebody Else, the Great One, the Great Parent, is always there. That One sees everything you do and represents a Parental Will relative to what you do. That One wants you to do certain things, wants you not to do other things, and will presumably reward you if you do the things that It wants you to do and will punish you in various ways if you do not do those things. Out of this kind of Parent-Godism come all the other traditions associated with the notions of sin, or the valuation of events not merely factually but in terms of the Parental Deity. In other words, if something negative happens to you, it is generally regarded as a Divinely given punishment or a result of what you have done in terms of your social personality and your conventional, moral activity. If good things happen to you, they are presumed to be gifts or rewards from the same Source.

Examine the point of view of conventional "downtown" religion—Christian religion, Jewish religion, Muslim religion. You must see that it basically corresponds to this structure of notions and is therefore primarily a development of our infantile state of awareness. It is a development of the original parent bond of our childhood, and it is complicated by the dissociative individuation that develops in adolescence and that tends to characterize our adulthood as well.

The Way that I consider with you is not a development of this childish or conventional religion. When I speak of God (and I also use other terms than "God," but this is one of the forms of reference I use), I am not speaking of this Parental Deity. I have frequently had occasion to criticize this childish way of relating to such terms and to the whole process of religion and spiritual life. I could compare the point of view that I consider with you to this childish religious point of view by saying that true religion is not founded in the primitive feeling that even when you are alone there is always Someone Else present. Rather, I describe the basis of true religion as a mysterious experience or intuition that no matter how many others are present, no matter how many people are present including yourself, no matter what is arising, there is only One Reality, One Self, One Condition. That One is not "other." That One is not your parent. And, in phenomenal and experiential terms, that One is not merely devoted to rewarding and punishing you, supporting you and protecting you. Rather, that One is manifested as all kinds of phenomenal conditions, opposites, even contradictions. We cannot account for that One in childish terms.

In fact, if we really examine the nature of Nature, or of phenomenal existence, there is no justification for believing in the Parental Deity at all. I would say there is zero justification for it. But this is for you to consider. Where is the justification for it? It is simply not true to the facts of existence altogether that there is a great, omniscient, omnipresent, omnipotent Being making everything happen, in charge of everything happening and making things turn out well for those who acknowledge that One and obey certain moral principles. It is simply not so. It is not so that there is such a Parental Deity controlling history, working out a great plan for humanity, making a great revelation of Truth historically once and for all, as in the case of Jesus or some other prophet or great figure.

The Divine, or God, the One to be Realized, is not other than ourselves. That One transcends our personal, conditional existence, but our conditional existence arises in that One. All of this is a modification of that One, a play upon that One. To Realize that One, we must enter profoundly into the Self-Position, not by means of the traditional method of inversion or of turning attention inward. I need not at this juncture go into my reasons for criticizing that particular effort, except to indicate that it is simply one of the ego-based solutions to a presumed problem of existence. But that criticism aside, That which we must Realize is in the Self-Position. And we Realize It not by appeal to Something outside ourselves nor by entering into childish dependence relative to some great Principle, but by transcending the limits on the Self-Position and Realizing the ultimate Potency of That in which we inhere.

Now all of this public chat, this seemingly endless conversation, about whether there is God or not is simply a continuation of the doubting and subjective mulling over of problem-consciousness that is part of the adolescence of mankind. Always wondering about whether there is God is simply an adult occupation of basically adolescent personalities who started to think that there is a God in the first place when they were children. This wondering about whether there is God is basically an effort to prove the existence of the God we believed in when we were children. But the God we believed in when we were children does not exist, not as it was then described to us, nor as we then believed. What we are told about what is said to be God when we are children is said in terms that our parents hope will satisfy our needs as children. In other words, parents develop our God-consciousness or our religious orientation when we are children as an extension of what they themselves are otherwise trying to do as parents. Parents naturally want their children to feel protected. They do not want them to become neurotic and to feel threatened. And they want their children to learn how to behave. They want them to develop socializing tendencies, to learn how to relate to others positively and to function socially, how to survive socially and in ordinary human terms. This is what parents want us to do, and, in some ordinary sense, it is natural enough for them to want us to do this. Thus, when parents teach religion to their children, as a general rule they teach them about a God who is basically a poetic extension of themselves as parents.

We do not want our children to feel unprotected, but really the source of their protection is ourselves, their parents, and the community, the human world. Apart from whatever protection we can generate for our children as their parents and as the community that surrounds them, they really are not very well protected. And neither are we! Beyond what we can do for one another as human beings cooperating together, there is very little protection in this world for any of us. So we do want our children to feel protected, but we are protecting them. There is no reason to invent a Santa Claus Parent-God to make them feel protected. We should let them know that we are protecting them, that we are providing them with circumstances wherein they will be able to live and not be threatened, and wherein they are loved quite naturally by others.

Really, children should understand that becoming a positive social personality is not supposed to be a way of getting the goods from God or getting love from "the Parent." In that syndrome, love is different from your own social activity, and your social activity is a way of getting love. What we should be teaching our children is that to become a social personality or a relational personality means that you become love. You must become love. Human beings must become loving. And social activities are not supposed to be something you do in order to get love. They should be love. The whole notion of sin and violation of the ultimate Parent is not something we need to communicate to our children.

You do not become truly religious unless you truly understand this Teaching and Awaken to its point of view. The Parental God of childish religion cannot be proven. That

One does not exist. The struggle to prove the existence of such a One is a false struggle. It is an expression of the common disease, the problem-consciousness of threatened egoity. This does not mean that we should all become like atheistic psychiatrists and throw religion away. Much of what is called religion should be thrown away, based on a very intelligent consideration, because it is just a man-made consolation for rather childish egos. But there is much more to true religion than what is contained in these childish propositions. It is that which goes beyond these childish propositions that I call you to consider in the form of my own Teaching and also in the evidence of the Great Tradition, or the total global inheritance of human culture.

There is the Great Being, the Great Divine Reality. There is that Truth. And there is a way of entering into the Realization of that One. It requires great maturity, not childishness, not adolescence, not egoity, and it involves the transcendence of everything conventionally religious that is associated with our childish and adolescent personality. We enter into that Realization not by appealing to the Other Power, the objective Parental Deity outside us, as proposed by conventional religion. The Way does not even involve appeal to that Great Other One in the form of mystical or subtle objects of any kind. The God who does not exist is not just the white-bearded Character of the *Old Testament* myths or, more precisely, of popular Judeo-Christian mythology. He is not even doing the same thing as that great-bearded One but is a kind of all-pervading Parentlike Essence. The God Who does exist is not present as a separate Personality in any exclusive sense anywhere in Nature. Nor is that One to be identified with any subtle object in Nature, or with any of the lights observable via mystical consciousness. We only Realize and, therefore, ultimately prove the existence of that One by entering most profoundly into the Self-Domain, the Self-

Position, the domain of our simple Existence, Is-ness, Being itself.

The God of Nature, the Creator God, cannot be proven because that One does not exist as proposed. But the Great God is Transcendental and exists in the Self-Position Transcendentally. In other words, It exists at the level of our eternal Existence and not at the level of the objects related to our conditional egoic existence, our manifest independence. This same One is also present to us in the form of all others, all objects, all states of nature—not as other, but rather as that One in which we inhere. That One is present as the Adept, the human Agent or Transmitter, but not in any exclusive sense, not as the Holy Other, but as That which manifests the Power of the Self-Position, the Transcendental Condition. That One is present as Spiritual Force, transmitted through Baptism and Good Company. And the purpose of Spiritual Baptism or reception of an Adept's Transmission, therefore, is to lead us into the Realization of That which is in the Self-Position. Its purpose is not to call us to conform to an apparent Power outside ourselves that requires us to engage in activities very similar to the childish social routines of conventional religiosity.

Thus, the Truth that is to be Realized may be summarized simply as the Realization that no matter what is arising, no matter how many others are present, there is only One Being. This is precisely different from the childish proposition that even when you are alone there is always Someone Else present.

February 7, 1983

God and Doubt

People today talk about God as if one could thoroughly deny that God Exists. The puzzlement about whether or not God Exists is not a true question at all. There is no genuine doubt that God Exists. Obviously you did not create yourself, nor can you sustain yourself independently, nor can you spontaneously uncreate yourself. You can only be confused by illusions of doubt, and these illusions can create the sense of separation from the Living Divine. Such doubts are only illusions whereby we become self-possessed, self-destructive, loveless, and incapable of Ecstasy.

We are lived. We are part of a Great Process that is ultimately mysterious, a Process in which we do not know. God, or the Inherent and Transcendental Reality, clearly Exists. Each of us is inherently obliged to relate to the Divine through love and to fulfill the Law of sacrifice that is Revealed to us in every moment of existence. The Divine Reveals Itself, in our sacrifice, through intuitive illumination, and through a process of psycho-physical transformation and ultimate Translation of self into the Real. Only the Awakened devotee truly understands or Realizes the Nature of God, the Reality of God.

There is no justifiable reason to doubt the Divine Reality. Doubt is simply a reflection of ourselves, our reluctance to fulfill the Law of sacrifice and to become Lawfully oriented to Infinity. Doubts about whether or not God exists are descriptions of Man in his recoil from Infinity. Impenetrable doubt cannot be logically justified in the midst of things. Concepts or beliefs about "God" may be doubted, but

Reprinted from *Scientific Proof of the Existence of God Will Soon Be Announced by the White House!* by Da Free John (The Dawn Horse Press, 1980).

that which is Divine and Eternal is always perfectly obvious—and, therefore, inherently beyond the conventional disposition we feel as doubt.

You are always "capable" of doubt, because doubt is a condition of yourself. It is a form of contraction. And when you involve yourself in contraction, you become mad—neither relational nor ecstatic. You have no clarity, no understanding, no capacity to transcend your own reactivity and isolation. Find yourself in that position, and then you start wondering if God is Real or if God Exists. But God is Reality. God is Existence. The mind may know doubt, but it cannot know what God, or Reality, or Existence is. The Divine is, therefore, beyond knowledge and doubt, which are only ordinary conventions of mind and experience. The Divine is Realized only through ecstasy, or self-transcendence, beyond knowledge and doubt. The Living God may be neither doubted nor known, but only Realized. God may only be loved.

Therefore, hear the critical argument of this Way of Radical Understanding or Divine Ignorance. Through Awakening to the intuition of the Divine, the unprovable and undoubtable Divine is simply, tacitly obvious. God is simply Reality. God is the Process of Existence altogether, and God ultimately Transcends the Process and the manifestations of all manifest experience.

March 23, 1978

The Existence of God Can Be Doubted, but Not Proven

Academic philosophers continue to persist in the silliest kind of sophomoric debates about the "existence of God." The arguments still range between the "proof" offered by Reason and the "proof" offered by Revelation—but both kinds of "proof" are nothing more than the poor servants of the adolescent dilemma of "rationalism."

To ask if God exists is already to doubt God's existence absolutely—and it reflects a commitment to the presumption that God does not exist until it is absolutely proven otherwise. Once it is presumed that the existence of God is in doubt or in need of proof, the dreadful dilemma of separation from God has already solidified, and neither inner Reason nor outer Revelation has sufficient Power to liberate the individual from the subtle and fundamental despair that is inherent in Godlessness.

I am in a different Mood, which I also propose to you. The most fundamental Mood of Man is one in which God, or the Living Divine Truth, is presumed to be obvious. God must be Realized as the obvious, not proven to exist. We must abide in the Mood of God-Realization, or inherence in the obvious, rather than that subhuman mood or irreducible dilemma wherein the obvious Truth must be proven to exist. We must proceed on the basis of prior inherence in God, or ecstatic surrender of the psycho-physical self in God, rather than on the basis of mental and physical separation from God. We must Realize God through our inherent, fundamental, and absolute Ignorance, rather than seek to prove or return to God through accumulations of knowledge and experience.

Reason and Revelation are the gods of separated and

Reprinted from *Scientific Proof of the Existence of God Will Soon Be Announced by the White House!* by Da Free John (The Dawn Horse Press, 1980).

self-possessed Man. Only Ignorance itself makes possible the direct Realization of God. And only those who first Realize and then constantly surrender to the Only, Living, and Obvious Divine are also capable of right understanding of the experiential processes of the body-mind.

The search for proof of the existence of God is really a search for reasons to be Happy. But the existence of God cannot be "proven" to the point of ecstasy, or the awakening of the opposite of irreducible doubt. The question "Does God exist or not?" is itself a proposition—it is doubt, it is the idea of separation from ecstatic Fullness, it is the self-image of Narcissus, it is the emotional contraction of the body-mind from God, Life, and all relations.[1] Reasons and Revelations are only a hedge around the pond of Narcissus—a false sanctuary for the wounded self, who presumes himself to be trapped in the dead ends of the Machine of Nature.

Only the Realization of God is the unique and actual healing of the self-bound and heart-wounded Man. And to Realize God we must first enjoy profound insight into the irreducible dilemma behind all our questions, which means we must confess the awful despair that lingers in us even in the face of all our answers. On the basis of that insight we are able to perceive that there is no inherent doubt or separate self, and we will thus Realize the Radiant Transcendental Being that is obvious prior to the functional contraction of the body-mind.

April 6, 1980

1. Narcissus, the self-lover of Greek mythology, is a key symbol in Master Da Free John's description of Man as a self-possessed seeker, enamored with what he does not recognize as his own image, one who suffers in dilemma, contracted upon himself at every level of the being from all relations and from the condition of relationship itself. "He is the ancient one visible in the Greek 'myth,' who was the universally adored child of the gods, who rejected the loved-one and every form of love and relationship, who was finally condemned to the contemplation of his own image, until he suffered the fact of eternal separation and died in infinite solitude." (*The Knee of Listening,* by Da Free John, p. 26)

Does God Exist?

God is evident in the dimension of Being, not of causes and effects!

The "question" of the existence of God is commonly posed relative to the evidence represented by the effects that may be perceived or the causes that may be presumed in the realm of Nature. Therefore, no ultimately satisfactory or deeply convincing proofs are offered by this approach.

The question "Does God exist?" is not truly a question. It is an expression of a confused or un-Enlightened state of human being. It is at once the evidence of that state and an emotional or psychic proposition based on that state. It is a question only in its outer form or linguistic expression. It is not a true question seeking an answer, nor can it be satisfactorily answered through any of the procedures that are traditionally suggested as responses to it as a question. It is simply a traditional rhetorical device, a literary instrument for communicating the presumption of doubt.

Real questions are gestures toward an answer. They are the ground of real enterprises. False or fake questions are merely symptoms of failed seeking. They seem to invite the search for an answer, but they truly function to undermine the motion of serious enquiry. They are themselves a neurotic or motionless stand point. Emotionally, they are the results of previous failed enquiry, rather than the initiators of new and future enquiry.

This pseudo-question "Does God exist?" (and similar renditions of the same proposition) has occupied, and still occupies, millions upon millions of un-Realized or un-

Reprinted from *"I" Is the Body of Life* by Da Free John (The Dawn Horse Press, 1981).

Enlightened human beings. It is one of the principal signs of the futility of conventionally outer-directed or materialistic philosophy and culture. It is an Idol made of words, made to stand in every marketplace, causing all who pass to knit the brow as if engaged in serious reflection. But the expression on those faces is merely one of bewilderment and frustrated intelligence.

The "question" in regard to God's existence is merely a verbal form of fundamental doubt. It is a proposition based on the prior assumption of egoic existence (or self-contraction in the Infinite Field of Being) in a world in which objects (or all that is not-self) are chronically presumed to be Reality, while beings and the Being that includes and transcends all beings and things are regarded to be non-existent as such. (That is, beings and Being are regarded to be merely variations on objective Nature, or even false conceptions or presumptions about Nature, and so, as such, they are un-Real.) Thus, the "question" is truly a symptomatic bit of evidence for the previous assumption of egoity and materialism. And all who struggle with the question are merely tussling with their own self-possessed doubt. No "answer" in the usual sense, both affirmative and convincing, ever comes of that struggle. There will always be the psychological residue of doubt. The "answer" will always include and express and confirm doubt. The "question" is actually a negative proposition relative to its subject. It is based on the prior denial of the existence of God. The "question" is merely a sign that the being (or the state of mind) that asks it is in question, in a state of alienation from Being, fixed upon causes and effects—conscious of Nature but unconscious of Being.

Such is the correct understanding of the traditional "ultimate question." It is not a true question (to be made the source of an enquiry that can possibly lead to a positive or affirmative answer in response). It is a false or pseudo-question, a symptom of dis-ease, a negative proposition hidden (but nonetheless made effective) in the form of a conventional open-ended question. Such pseudo-questions must first of all be recognized as such. And this is the key: The secret of how to deal with false questions is to recognize them as such, and so transcend them rather than seek to answer them.

It is time for us to cease to take this question "seriously," as we must in general abandon our serious embrace of the structure and destiny of egoic existence and its materialistic philosophy, alienated from Transcendental Being and confined to the illusion that the objective not-self is, in itself, Reality. The traditional "ultimate question" is not a true question seeking an answer. It is, when embraced as a true question, merely a proposition that priorly establishes only one possible answer (which is negative and also not the Truth). Questions of such a kind must be transcended in order for the Truth to be affirmed by Realization.

Such questions are actually forms of what the Japanese call the "ko-an." The "ko-an" is an apparent question—that is, we tend to try to answer it via the usual operations of mind. But the "question" itself works to undermine the mental process. It is actually a form of meditation on doubt, or failed mind. Therefore, the "ko-an" is "answered" only when it is transcended as a motivator of thought. When its power to initiate doubt and confine us to doubt is understood and transcended, then there is a sudden rush of joy, freedom, and tacit Intuition of Transcendental Being.

The pseudo-question "Does God exist?" is actually a "ko-an," a primary "ko-an" of the Western mind. And it is only through understanding and transcending it that Western civilization (and the beings affected by the dogmatic illusions of separate self and objective Nature or Reality) will Awaken to the sanity of Truth.

All ultimate pseudo-questions must be understood and transcended in this manner. But such understanding and transcendence may require great struggle (as is traditionally the case with "ko-an" meditation), since a profound transformation of the fundamental context of knowledge and experience is required. No mere mental logic can produce liberation from the "ko-an."

Actually, all "ko-ans" or ultimate pseudo-questions are absurd propositions. But great intuitive insight (into the body-mind-self as well as the apparent "question") is required for such to be really understood. The "ko-an" "Does God exist?" is actually the absurd propositional question "Does Reality exist, or only the Un-Real?" The use of the word "God" tends to cause us to forget that the "question" is an invitation to consider the Reality or Truth of Nature and the Nature or Truth of Reality. Whatever ultimately exists is, by definition, Reality. The "Un-Real" cannot exist (although it can seem to be presumed or proposed). The hidden negative proposition in the "ko-an" or pseudo-question "Does God exist?" is: "Reality does not exist, only the Un-Real exists." It is an absurd proposition, but we tend to take it seriously, until true understanding Awakens.

The struggle with a "ko-an" is traditionally initiated by honest or rightly purposive Teachers who place them on their students' minds the way a dishonest merchant places a heavy finger on a scale to make his patrons believe they have been given a full weight. The materialistic and ego-based mind of the traditional West (and of un-Enlightened beings, East or West) has been saddled with this illusory burden of the "ultimate question" for so long, or under such circumstances, that neither a Teacher nor a Teaching is presumed under all this. Only the burden of the weight is on our minds. Therefore, understand. The "ko-an" is intended to initiate a struggle that will frustrate temporarily but also ultimately lead to the conversion of being. The ultimate conversion is from psycho-physical egoity (and materialistic presumptions about Reality) to Being (or Transcendental Freedom, prior to all the illusory burdens of presumed knowledge and conventional experience).

The Real exists. The Real is all that exists, and only what exists. The Real is not exclusively outside the self (in the context of objects, relations, or all that is not-self), for then It would not include whatever is self. Nor is the Real exclusively inside the self, for then It would not include whatever is apparently related to the self. The Real is the Ultimate Context of the self and its relations. It includes and transcends whatever is the self and all its possible relations. The Real is not merely in the context of objects, or materiality, or what is bodily known and experienced. The Real is equally in the context of mind, psyche, being, and also all that is beyond knowledge and experience. Even Nature is to be understood as a total psycho-physical process and not merely an objective, physical, or material one. Truly, the Real is the Context that includes all and thus transcends every particularity. The Real is Realized only in self-transcendence, surrender, or free participation, to the degree of ultimate transcendence. The Real is "known" only in Ignorance, or the Realization (in relation to any present appearance) that "I" do not know what it is. To Realize the Real is, therefore, to transcend "I" (or the self-contraction) and its relations (or the conventional presumptions of knowledge and experience relative to whatever presently appears).

The Real is God. God is the Real. The Real exists. Therefore, God exists. God or Reality is Existence. Everything that exists expresses a Single Mystery, which is Existence or Being Itself. To enjoy such an Intuition of Existence is to Worship and Realize God in Truth, as very Existence or Transcendental Being, Consciousness, and Love-Bliss. The

Real is the Transcendental Identity and Condition of self (or the subject) and not-self (or all objects and conditions). Therefore, God is That Self-Identity and Condition, Which is Transcendental Consciousness and Unqualified Love-Bliss, the Nature of Nature and the Identity or Ultimate Condition of the body-mind-self. This is to be Realized via the struggle or sacred ordeal with the conventions of the body-mind-self, its objects, relations, or conditions, and its presumed knowledge and experience. And that struggle or sacred ordeal—rather than any conventional philosophizing, thinking, presuming, seeking, or experiencing—is the spiritual Way of Life, or the Way that I Teach.

Those who Realize God, Reality, or Truth beyond question (or doubt) are those whose fixation upon self and Nature, or the Play of causes, effects, knowledge, and experience, is suspended or transcended in the prior Intuition of Radiant Transcendental Being. However this may have happened in their case, they proclaim and demonstrate a certainty that God, or Transcendental Being, is the Nature of Nature, the Condition of all conditions, the Matrix of all appearances, the Radiant Reality in which Nature and all beings are arising. (Those who have not thus transcended the binding power of self and Nature wear doubt, literally, in their hearts and minds, and they always contemplate its terrible message.)

Based on the Confession made by those who have found the Domain of Being, others (who are yet fixed upon Nature, cause, effect, and the self that knows and experiences causes and effects) become hopeful, or fascinated with the possibility of God. And so they try to develop arguments that prove the existence of God, based on the suggestiveness of Nature's order, or the presumption of an Ultimate Cause, and so forth. They may even regard the historical appearance of one or more extraordinary individuals (whose Intuition and Radiant demonstration of Being was great) as proof of the existence of God. But all such efforts and their arguments are fruitless, since final proof of the existence of God cannot be presumed on the basis of any argument relative to causes and effects. The only proof of the existence of God is in the unmediated Intuition of Radiant Transcendental Being.

Therefore, those who have Awakened to the Intuition of Being have tried to direct others toward this Intuition, usually through a discipline that involves an ecstatic turning away from fixed attention to causes and effects (or conditional awareness of Nature) coupled with an enstatic turning into the Intuition of Being (prior to the conventions of self, mind, body, and their objects or relations).

There are many variations on this basic approach to be found in the religious and sacred traditions of mankind. And the kinds of approach may generally be understood to belong to the conventions that I have described in terms of the fourth, fifth, and sixth stages of life.[1] Therefore, many

1. Master Da Free John has described the development or spiritual evolution of the human individual in terms of seven stages. The first five stages of life include what we conventionally conceive to be the human, religious, and spiritual development of Man. The first three stages develop the physical, emotional, and mental functions of the body-mind and the corresponding expressions of secular culture and exoteric religion. The fourth stage of life is the stage of heartfelt surrender and profound intimacy with the Spirit. Thus, those who attain to the fourth stage of life practice religion in its freest sense. The fifth stage represents the secret or esoteric culture of initiates in all ancient traditions. Those who attain to the fifth stage of life exploit the yoga of the central nervous system, what Master Da sometimes refers to as "brain mysticism," as the path to higher knowledge.

From the point of view of the sixth and seventh stages of life, the first five stages are a culture of progressive disciplines devoted to releasing energy and attention from worldly preoccupation with the fulfillment of the functions of the body-mind, and the process of the first five stages is considered to be preparation for the primary and direct exercises of intuitive insight and intuition of the Transcendental or Unconditional Reality. The sixth stage Teaching has therefore traditionally been offered to highly advanced practitioners for whom the consideration or contemplation of uncommon forms of experience and presumed knowledge have become identified with the Realization of God.

Magical, mystical, and highly evolved yogic or psychic states particularly common to fourth and fifth stage practices have become associated with Ultimate Realization in the religious and spiritual traditions. But such uncommon or extraordinary phenomena are no more a form of evidence or proof of the existence of God than the conventional intellectual arguments relative to Nature in general. That is, phenomenal states of experience and presumed knowledge are themselves part of the Play of Nature, or of causes and effects. Therefore, the achievement of such states is no more direct or consequential to the certainty and Free Happiness of God-Realization than mere intellectual arguments without extraordinary experience.

The only proof of the existence of God is in the unmediated Intuition of Radiant Transcendental Being, free of all dependence on the body-mind, and utterly transcending the separate or conditional and contracted self. Only on the basis of such Intuition is Transcendental Being tacitly Realized

---

Consciousness is a viable discipline. But the seventh or God-Realized stage of life transcends all subject-object consciousness, including the strategic manipulation of attention to invert upon the self-essence, which characterizes the sixth stage of life.

Master Da writes of the seventh stage:

In the seventh stage of life there is native or radical intuitive identification with the Radiant Transcendental Being, the Identity of all beings (or subjects) and the Condition of all conditions (or objects). This intuitive identification (or Radical Self-Abiding) is directly Realized, entirely apart from any dissociative act of inversion. And, while so Abiding, if any conditions arise, or if any states of body-mind arise, they are simply recognized in the Radiant Transcendental Being (as transparent or non-binding modifications of Itself).

The seven stages of eternal life are discussed in greater detail in Appendix A of *The Fire Gospel: Essays and Talks on Spiritual Baptism* by Da Free John, which also includes a bibliography of Master Da Free John's instructions on the seven stages.

to be the Real-Condition or Identity of Nature and the egoic self. Even the sixth stage error of exclusive inwardness must be transcended at last, in the Intuition of Being as the Identity and Condition of self and Nature. (Such is the seventh stage Realization, in Sahaj Samadhi,[2] and, by this Realization, all of self and Nature is ultimately transcended or Outshined, in Bhava Samadhi,[3] or perfect Translation.)

Thus, we must at least gradually transcend our fixation upon self and Nature, causes and effects, knowledge and experience. We are all inevitably drawn to seek Happiness, and as we seek we achieve progressively more profound levels of experience and presumed knowledge. Each time such a new level is attained, it is inspected and, ultimately, found wanting (or insufficient for unqualified Happiness). Only when all conditional possibilities, high or low in the scale of Nature, lose their power to attract us (as if Happiness were in their achievement) do we fall into the unmediated Intuition of Being and Realize the Radiant Truth that Transcends Nature.

Those whose "hearing"[4] of the Transcendental Argument of the Adept is relatively immature begin their reorientation to the Divine or Radiant Transcendental Being more

2. Sahaj Samadhi is the "open eyed" or natural state, in which whatever arises is seen to be only the modification of the prior Divine Condition, or the natural disposition of clear Identification with the Transcendental Self or Being rather than the self-contraction in any sense.

3. Bhava Samadhi is the realized state of the most radical enjoyment prior to self, mind, body, energy, or any realm. It is the Condition of conditions, existence in the Condition or "Realm" that is Only God, the very Reality. It is without or prior to references, and it is, therefore, unspeakable, or without description.

4. "Hearing" is a technical term used by Master Da Free John to describe the intuitive understanding of the self-contraction and simultaneous intuitive awakening to Divine Consciousness that arise on the basis of disciplined study of the argument of the Adept. Only on the basis of such hearing can the practice of true spiritual life begin.

slowly and on the basis of the struggle with disciplines of the lower self. Those whose "hearing" is more profound readily achieve equanimity of the body-mind and enjoy greater freedom of energy and attention for the radical process of Ultimate Intuition (although they may be at least briefly distracted by the subtle phenomena of the higher self or mind). Those whose "hearing" is (or at least eventually becomes) most profound are stably founded in psycho-physical equanimity (free of the distracting or binding power of the lower and the higher functions of the manifest conditional self), and their energy and attention are completely free for the direct or unmediated Intuition of Transcendental Being (beyond all objects and beyond inversion upon the internal self-essence).

Human existence, even the existence of all beings apparent in Nature, is a sacred ordeal of seeking for Happiness, or of return to Identification with Transcendental Being. Once Transcendental Being is perfectly Realized, the cause and effect Play of Nature becomes transparent, unnecessary, and without binding power. The egoic self, manifest as experience and presumed knowledge in the body-mind and in association with countless objects and relations, is likewise transcended and Realized to be transparent, unnecessary, and without binding power. In the unmediated or radical Intuition and perfect or final Realization of Radiant Transcendental Being, God is Obvious as the Identity, Condition, and Reality of Nature, all causes and effects, and all beings. In that Realization Consciousness, rather than objective Nature, is found to be the Reality of existence. And that Consciousness which is Transcendental Being is Eternal Ignorance, or Radiant Love-Bliss, Inherently and always already free. God is not the mere Cause of causes, the conventional Parental Creator of effects. God is not the mere God of Nature. God is Transcendental Being, Infinite

Consciousness, and Eternal Radiance or Love-Bliss, the Condition of Nature (not merely its Creator) and the Identity of beings (not merely their Parent and Controller).

The Teaching and the Company of an Adept (one whose Realization of Radiant Transcendental Being is perfect, unmediated, and most profound) is traditionally valued above all other means or guides to the Realization of Truth, God, Reality, or Happiness, because such Teaching and Company are the only true convincing Testimony, the most perfect Demonstration, the surest and most direct Guide, and the most potent Agent of Transmission. Those who are serious in the commitment to this Realization and who "hear" the Teaching truly, value such Teaching and cultivate such Company above all. They quickly achieve humor and responsibility relative to their own conventions of self. They see through and beyond all appearances, they delight in the Awakened Company of the Adept, and they quickly transcend all false evidence and all conditional distractions.

May all beings be Blessed with such quickness.

November 18, 1981

God as the Creator, the Good, and the Real

Conventional religion originates in the consciousness that characterizes the earlier stages of life. Thus, it is ego-based and it serves the functional desire of the manifest or phenomenal self to be protected, nourished, pleasurized, and ultimately preserved.

The phenomenal self or egoic (self-centered) body-mind is the source of conventional religion as well as all of the other ordinary and extraordinary pursuits of born-existence in the first six stages of life. Therefore, it is not God but the ego (perhaps gesturing conceptually toward God) that is the source and fundamental subject of popular religion as well as higher mysticism. Real spirituality, true religion, or Transcendental Occupation begins only when the egoic-consciousness (with all of its mind, emotion, desire, and activity) is thoroughly understood and inherently transcended. For this reason, only the radical Teaching of the Wisdom of the seventh stage of life directly serves the process of actual God-Realization. All other forms of doctrine or instruction serve the purposes of the first six stages of life—all of which are founded on manifest egoity and conditional attention.

It is the culture of conventional religion that promotes the conventional ideas about God. The principal conventional God-idea is that God is the Creator (or intentional Emanator) of the worlds and all beings. Such seems an obvious idea to the bodily ego, trapped in the mechanics of the perceptual mind and the material or elemental vision. The ego is identified with embodiment, and the idea of the Creator-God

Reprinted from *Nirvanasara: Radical Transcendentalism and the Introduction of Advaitayana Buddhism*, by Da Free John (The Dawn Horse Press, 1982).

is developed to account for this fact and to provide a conceptual basis (in the form of the idea of the ego as God-made creature) for the appeal to God to Help the ego in this world and in the yet unknown after-death state.

The difficulty with the Creator-God conception is that it identifies God with ultimate causation and thus makes God inherently responsible for the subsequent causation of all effects. And if God is responsible for all effects, then God is clearly a very powerful but also terrible Deity—since manifest existence tends to work equally for and against all creatures.

Therefore, the Creator-God idea is commonly coupled with the idea of God as Good (and thus both opposite and opposed to Evil). If the Creator-God is conceived to be Good (or always working to positively create, protect, nourish, rightly and pleasurably fulfill, and ultimately preserve all of Nature and all creatures), then the ego is free of the emotional double-bind and the anger and despair that would seem to be justified if God is simply the responsible Creator of everything (good, evil, bad, or in between). Therefore, conventional theology, most especially as it has tended to develop under the influence of the Semitic religions of the Middle East, is founded on the ideas of God as Creator and God as Good (or Good Will).

But if God is the all-powerful Creator (without whom not anything has been made), then how did so much obviously negative or evil motion and effect come into existence? The usual answer is generally organized around one or another mythological story in which powerful creatures (or one powerful creature, such as the Devil, now regarded to personify Evil) entered (on the basis of free will) into a pattern of "sin," or disobedience and conflict with God, which resulted in separation from God and a descent or fall into material consciousness, and so forth. Such mythologies are structured in terms of a hierarchical view of Nature, with various planes descending from the Heaven of God. Religion thus becomes a method of return to God.

Exoteric religion is generally based on an appeal to belief, social morality, and magical prayer or worship. The return to God is basically conceived in terms of this world and, therefore, exoteric or terrestrial religion is actually a process in which God returns to the ego and to this world (rather than vice versa), and it is believed that God will eventually reclaim mankind and the total world from the forces of Evil. But exoteric religion is an outer cult, intended for grosser egos and for mass consumption (or the culture of the first three stages of life). The ultimate form of conventional religion is in the esoteric or inner and sacred cult, which is a mystical society, open only to those chosen for initiation (and thus growth or evolution into the fourth and fifth stages of life). Esoteric religion is a process of cosmic mysticism, or the method of return to God by ascending as mind (or disembodied soul), back through the route of the original fall into matter and Evil, until the Heaven or Eternal Abode of God is reached again. The esoteric religious process goes beyond the conventions of exoteric religion to develop the psycho-physical mechanics of mystical flight and return to God via the hierarchical structures of the nervous system (ascending from the plane of Evil, or the Devil, or the "flesh," at the bodily base of the nervous system, to the plane of the Good, or God, or the Heavenly Abode, at or above the brain, via the "magic carpet" of the life-force in the nervous system).

Thus, the idea of the Creator-God leads to the idea that God is Good (or the Good Will), which leads to the idea that creatures have free will, which then accounts for the appearance of sin, suffering, evil, and loss of God-consciousness. And conventional religion then becomes the means (through structures of belief, sacramental worship, mystical prayer, yogic or shamanistic ascent, and so forth) for the re-exercise of creaturely free will in the direction of God, Good, the triumph over Evil and death in this world, and the ascent from material form and consciousness to spiritual, heavenly, or Godly form and consciousness.

All the popular and mystical religious and spiritual traditions of mankind tend to be associated with this chain of conceptions (or the characteristic ideas of the first five stages of life). It is only in the sixth and seventh stage traditions that these ideas begin to give way to different conceptions. It is only in the sixth stage of life that the egoic basis of the first five stages of life is penetrated. And it is only in the seventh stage of life that the ego is altogether transcended in the Real Divine.

The theological and general religious conceptions I have just described have always been subject to criticism (or at least simple non-belief) on the part of those who are not persuaded by religious and theological arguments. Atheism has always opposed theism. But atheistic ideas are the product of the same fundamental self-consciousness that otherwise produces theistic or conventional religious ideas. Atheism is the product of the ego (or the phenomenal self, grounded in elemental perception), and so also is theism. Atheism, like exoteric religion, extends itself only into the domain of the first three stages of life, whereas esoteric religion and theism provide a means for entering, mystically and spiritually, into the evolution of the fourth and fifth stages of life.

Atheism regularly proposes a logical view of life that has its own dogmatic features. It does not propose a God-idea but, instead, founds itself on and in the perceptual and phenomenal mind alone. Atheism concedes only a universal and ultimately indifferent (or merely lawful) Nature (not God), and so there is no need to create a religious "creation myth" to account for suffering. (And atheistic thinkers thus generally confine themselves to constructing a cosmology, based on material observations alone, that merely accounts for the appearance of the manifest events of Nature.) Indeed, just as conventional religion or theism arises to account for suffering, atheism arises on the basis of the unreserved acknowledgment of suffering. And if there is no idea of God, there is no idea of Man as creature (or Man as the bearer of an immortal or God-like inner part). Nor is there any need to interpret unfortunate or painful events as the effects of Evil. Therefore, the atheistic point of view is characterized by the trend of mind that we call "realism," just as the conventional religious or theistic point of view is characterized by the trend of mind that we call "idealism," but both atheism and theism arise on the basis of the self-contraction, or the ego of phenomenal self-consciousness, rather than on the basis of direct intuition of the Real Condition that is prior to self and its conventions of perception and thought.

The realistic or atheistic view is just as much the bearer of a myth (or a merely conceptual interpretation of the world) as is the conventional religious or theistic view. Atheism (or conventional realism) is a state of mind that is based in the phenomenal self and that seeks the ultimate protection, nourishment, pleasure, and preservation of the phenomenal self (at least in this world and, if there should be an after-life, then also in any other world). Therefore, it is simply an alternative philosophy to theism and conventional religion, based on the same principle and consciousness (the phenomenal ego), and seeking by alternative means to fulfill the manifest self and relieve it of its suffering.

Atheism, or conventional realism, is a state of mind that possesses individuals who are fixed in the first three stages of life. It is a form of spiritual neurosis (or self-possession), as are all of the characteristic mind-states of the first six stages of life. Esoteric religion and theism provide a basis for certain remarkable individuals to enter the fourth and fifth stages of life, but the commonly (or exoterically) religious individual is, like the atheist, a relatively adolescent (if not childish and even infantile) character, fixed in the egoic neuroses of the first three stages of life.

Atheism proposes a myth and a method for ego-fulfillment that is based on phenomenal realism, rather than spiritual idealism (or the culture of the conventional God-idea). Therefore, atheism is traditionally associated with the philosophy of materialism, just as theism is associated with spiritualism, animism, and Emanationism. And the realistic or atheistic view tends to be the foundation for all kinds of political, social, and technological movements, since its orientation is toward the investigation and manipulation of material Nature. Atheism is realism and materialism. It is about the acquisition of knowledge about Nature and the exploitation of that knowledge to command (or gain power over) Nature. And it is this scheme of knowledge and power (expressed as political and technological means of all kinds) that is the basis of the mythology and quasi-religion of atheism. The atheistic (or non-theistic) view of life is ego-based, organized relative to Nature as an elemental or perceived process, and committed to knowledge and power as the means of salvation (or material fulfillment of egoity).

In our time, this materialistic, realistic, and non-theistic philosophy of ego-fulfillment is represented by the world-culture of scientific, technological, and political materialism. The entire race of mankind is now being organized by the cultural movement of scientific materialism, while the alternative cultures of theism, mystical esotericism, sixth stage Transcendentalism, and the ultimate or truly radical philosophy of the seventh stage of life are tending to be systematically suppressed and propagandized out of existence. Scientism (or the culture of realistic or materialistic knowledge) and its two arms of power (technology and political order) are the primary forces in world-culture at the present time. And humanity at large is thus tending to be reduced to the robot acculturations of orderly egoism in the limited terms represented by our functional development in the first three stages of life.

Conventional and popular human culture has historically been limited to the conflicts and alternatives represented by theism and atheism, or egoic idealism and egoic realism. And the large scale ordering of mankind has always tended to be dominated by the politics of materialistic knowledge and power. It is simply that in the twentieth century we are seeing that materialistic culture approach the achievement of a world-wide mass culture in which all individuals will be controlled by a powerful and materialistically oriented system of political and technological restriction.

The usual or most commonly remarked criticism of theism is based on the evidence of suffering and material limitation. Therefore, the common arguments against religion and theism are generally those proposed by the point of view of atheism. Likewise, the common arguments against atheism are generally those proposed by theism (or an appeal to egoic acceptance of the evidence of religious history, cultic revelation, mystical psychology, and psychic experience). For this reason, there may seem to be only two basic cultural alternatives: atheism and theism.

But theism and religion are, at base, the expressions of egoity in the first three stages of life, just as is the case with atheism and conventional materialism. Therefore, whenever theism or religion becomes the base for political and social order, it inevitably becomes the base for knowledge and power in the material world. And theistic regimes have historically been equally as aggressive in the manipulation and suppression of humanity as have atheistic regimes. Theism is, at its base, egoic and fitted to worldly concerns. Therefore, when it achieves worldly power, it simply adopts the same general materialistic means that are adopted by atheism. Knowledge and power are the common tools of egoity, not merely the tools of atheism. It is simply that theism and religion can, via the exercises and attainments of saints and mystics, apply knowledge and power to purposes that extend beyond the first three stages of life. But in the terms of the first three stages of life (or the common and practical social order), theism and religion are inclined to make the same demands for social consciousness and to apply fundamentally the same kind of political and authoritarian techniques for achieving obedience and order as are applied by atheism and scientism.

This is evident in the popular theistic (and now almost exclusively exoteric) cultures that have come out of the Semitic tradition of the Middle East. Judaism, Christianity, and Islam are the principal theistic religions (in terms of worldly power and numbers), and they are all based on similar idealistic conceptions of God and creature and salvation, but each of these cults has also historically sought and achieved the general power to command the social order. And, in the process, each of these cults became a political State, controlling the forms of knowledge and power. As a result, over time these religions developed more and more of a secular, materialistic, and worldly character. Each of the three cults claims absolute, independent, and exclusive religious and worldly authority, and the historical conflict among these three (and between their claims and the equally absolutist and absurd claims of other and atheistic or non-religious systems, such as communism, democratic capitalism, and technological scientism) has now become the basis for idealistic State politics and political conflicts all over the world. And the seemingly more important or esoteric matters of spiritual wisdom, mystical knowledge, and the magical power of sainthood or Adeptship are as much in doubt and disrepute in the common religious circles of theism as they are in scientific and atheistic circles.

All of this is to indicate that conventional religion and theism share a root error or limitation with atheism and worldly culture. That error or limitation is the ego itself, or the presumptions and the seeking that are most basic to the conception of an independent phenomenal self in a less than hospitable phenomenal world. What is ultimately to be criticized in religion or theism is the same limit that is to be criticized in atheism and materialism. It is the ego, the phenomenal self-base, from which we tend to derive our conceptions of God, Nature, life, and destiny.

It is only when the egoic root of our functional, worldly, and religious or spiritual life is inspected, understood, and transcended that self, and world, and God are seen in Truth. Therefore, it is necessary to understand. It is necessary to aspire to Wisdom, Truth, and Enlightenment. All occupations derived from the ego-base are necessarily limited to egoity, and all conceptions that feed such egoic occupations are necessarily bereft of a right view of self, world, and God (or the ultimate and Transcendental Reality and Truth).

When the mechanics of egoity are transcended in our understanding, then it becomes obvious that life (or manifest phenomenal existence) is simply a play of opposites. Neither "Good" (or creation and preservation) nor "Evil" (or destruction) finally wins. Nature, in all its planes, is inherently a dynamic. The play of Nature, in all its forms and beings and processes, is not merely (or exclusively and finally) seeking the apparent "Good" of self-preservation (or the preservation and fulfillment of any particular form, world, or being), nor is it merely (or exclusively and finally) seeking the apparent "Evil" of self-destruction (or the dissolution of any particular form, world, or being). Rather, the play in Nature is always in the direction of perpetuating the dynamics of the play itself—and, therefore, polarity, opposition, struggle, alternation, death, and cyclic repetition tend to be perpetuated as the characteristics of phenomenal existence. Therefore, the play of Nature is always alternating between the appearance of dominance by one or the other of its two basic extremes. And the sign of this is in the inherent struggle that involves every form, being, and process. The struggle is this dynamic play of opposites, but the import of it is not the absolute triumph of either half. Things and beings and processes arise, they move, they are transformed, and they disappear. No thing or being or process is ultimately preserved. But neither is there any absolute destruction. Nature is a transformer, not merely a creator or a destroyer.

To the ego (or present temporary form of being) self-preservation may seem to be the inevitable motive of being. Therefore, a struggle develops to destroy or escape the dynamic of Nature by dominating Evil (or death) with Good (or immortality). This ideal gets expressed in the generally exoteric and occidental or more materialistic efforts to conquer Nature via worldly knowledge and power. But it also gets expressed in the more esoteric and oriental or mystical efforts to escape the plane of Nature by ascent from materiality (or the Evil of the flesh) to Heaven (the Good God above the consciousness of Nature).

But when the ego (or self-contraction) is understood and transcended, then Nature is seen from the point of view of Wisdom. And, in that case, the egoic struggle in Nature or against Nature is also understood and transcended. Then the Way of life ceases to be founded on the need to destroy the dynamic of Nature via conventional knowledge, power, immortality, or mystical escape. The world is no longer conceived as a drama of warfare between Good and Evil. The righteousness of the search for the Good as a means of self-preservation disappears along with the self-indulgent and self-destructive negativity of possession by Evil. In place of this dilemma of opposites, a self-transcending and world-transcending (or Nature-transcending) equanimity appears. And in that equanimity there is an inherent Radiance that transcends the egoic dualities of Good and Evil (or the conventional polarities of the self in Nature). It is the Radiance of Love. And in that Free Radiance, energy and attention are inherently free from the ego-bond, self-contraction, or the "gravitational effect" of phenomenal self-awareness. Therefore, dynamic equanimity, or the free disposition of Love (rather than the egoic disposition in the modes of Good or Evil), is the "window" through which God may be "seen" (or intuited)—not in the conventional mode of Creator, Good, Other, or Heavenly Place, but as the Real, or the tacitly obvious Condition of all existence.

The ultimate moment in the play of Nature is not the moment of egoic success (or the temporary achievement of the apparently positive or "Good" effect). The ultimate moment is beyond contradiction (or the dynamics of polarized opposites). It is the moment of equanimity, the still point or "eye" in the midst of the wheel of Nature's motions and all the motivations of the born self. The Truth and Real Condition of self and Nature is Revealed only in that equanimity, beyond all stress and bondage of energy and attention.

This disposition of equanimity (or free energy and attention) is basic to the conceptions of the sixth and seventh stages of life. In the sixth stage of life, it provides the functional base for the ultimate and final investigation of the ego and the dynamics of Nature. But in the seventh stage of life, fundamental equanimity is native and constant, expressing prior Transcendental Realization. It is in the seventh stage of life that God, Truth, or Reality is directly obvious, prior to every trace of egoity, dilemma, and seeking. Therefore, it is in the seventh stage of life that God is truly proclaimed, not in the conventional mode of Creator, or the Good, but as the Real. God is the Transcendental Truth, Reality, Identity, and Condition of self and Nature. In the seventh stage of life, That is tacitly obvious, and there is not anything that must be escaped or embraced for the Happiness of God-Realization to be actualized. It is inherently so. Therefore, the Way that I Teach is not any egoic means for attaining God-Realization. The Way is God-Realization Itself (prior to the methods of the first six stages of life). God, or the Transcendental Reality, prior to self, world, and the conventions of religion and non-religion, exotericism and esotericism, is the Way, the Truth, and the Life.

March 8, 1982

The Religious Ambivalence of Western Man

a talk by Da Free John

MASTER DA: There is something very negative implicit in the religious consciousness of Western people. "Is there a God?" seems to be the question you should be asking in order to become religious. But it is a completely absurd question. It has nothing whatever to do with spiritual life. It has to do with human beings, not with God. The question "Is there a God?" reflects a state in human beings for which they must be responsible. It is not itself a question that can be answered or that must be answered. But the religious consciousness of Western people is ambivalent. Westerners are very worldly and strong on the one hand, when religion permits worldliness, and on the other hand they are phasing, weak, always threatened at the level of subjective, or psychic, responsibility.

The Western consciousness is always trying to make positive whatever is overwhelmingly negative. The negative thing is what is powerful. We in the West are always trying to overcome it with positive feeling, with beliefs, with effort, with answers, with knowledge. The negative pattern, or karma,[1] is actually what is creating your life. Thus, people

Reprinted from *The Way That I Teach*, by Da Free John (The Dawn Horse Press, 1978).

1. Karma is action that entails consequences or re-actions. Thus, karma is destiny, tendency, the quality of existence that is determined by previous actions or conditions. And, by extension, karma is also latent tendencies, or patterns of action and reaction, condition and experience, that originate prior to and apart from the presently conscious mind.

remain characteristically weak, obsessed with an uninspected negative force that is always influencing their behavior and their thinking. They are always trying to surmount it through self-effort or association with the "Edible Deity"—the external Savior or God whose power they can consume irresponsibly. Therefore, faith and belief are reduced to ways of overcoming negativity.

In the Western doctrines (and the Middle Eastern teachings that gave rise to them) the negative force that tends to overwhelm us beneath the superficial mind is interpreted as sin, a disposition to be overcome by association with something greater than yourself—the Edible Deity, the Savior, the true God, the true religion, the true belief. Presuming a negative position, you orient yourself toward something positive and are saved by it. But you are still always sinful. You are always tending to fall back on sin.

The fundamental tenet of the Middle Eastern religions, Jewish or Christian or Islamic, is that this world and everything in it, including Man, is the creation of God. Man is also the highest creation of God, reflecting the Deity although not in any sense equal to the Deity. Therefore, the negative view of this life and this world is itself a form of sin. It is a sin to believe that this world is not godly, or that the Divine is not the ultimate destiny of the world, or that the world is not controlled by the Divine. The presumption of the West is that if the world is under the control of the Divine, its destiny is altogether positive, whatever its present condition may be. Therefore, to view the world negatively is itself sinful.

On the other hand, the strictly left-sided or classically Oriental point of view does not adhere to the principle that the world is the creation of God and that God is therefore its destiny.[2] The principle that is appealed to in the East

2. Master Da Free John has considered the divided self and culture of Man at length in such books as *The Enlightenment of the Whole Body* and *Scientific*

transcends phenomena, even excludes phenomena and precedes them altogether. The Oriental mind is critical of the world itself, not just of things in the world. The world is viewed not as the creation of God, but as an illusion. Thus, to view this world positively, in itself necessary, in itself the point of existence, rather than to transcend the world, is to be swept up in an illusion, a false point of view. That is sin, from the Oriental point of view. The natural disposition in the West is toward the world itself, to move into the world with a positive moral character, struggling against sin, the negative power. The natural disposition in the Orient is toward transcendence of this world.

From the Western, right-sided point of view, your association with the Edible Deity, the Savior, is what gives you strength. He gives you the Spirit. Through the magic of your association with this Savior, you acquire the spiritual force that enables you from moment to moment to overcome your own sinfulness and negativity so that you can participate in this great plan of creation. The Oriental, left-sided point of view has nothing whatever to do with such an idea (although clearly Western and Middle Eastern ideas have filtered into Oriental culture so that the later, more modern cultures and

---

Proof of the Existence of God Will Soon Be Announced by the White House! The right hemisphere of the brain naturally gives rise to primarily nonverbal, spatial, and holistic methods of relating to the objects of experience. It controls the left side of the body, and its qualities are most directly analogous to the ingoing (subjective) and upgoing (ascending) sensory currents of the body. These qualities typify in general the mystical and sacred cultures of the East. The left hemisphere of the brain naturally gives rise to the primarily verbal, temporal, and analytical methods of relating to the objects of experience. It controls the right side of the body, and its qualities are most directly analogous to the downgoing (descending) and outgoing (objective) motor currents of the body. The qualities of the "left brain" are, in general, typical of the scientific and materialistic cultures of the West. Master Da Free John Teaches that the limitations of these divisions of body, mind, and culture must be transcended and the whole body Enlightened through the practice of real or spiritual life.

traditions of the Orient tend to varying degrees to reflect that right-sided point of view). Therefore, when the disciple approached a traditional Spiritual Master in the East, he was not trying to find out how to live better—he was looking for liberation from the world. But the people who went to Jesus, or Mohammed, or Moses did not ask how to be liberated from the world. That was not their question. They wanted to be certain that there is God and that the one they were talking to was a true messenger of God. And then they wanted to know what they should be doing in order to enjoy the blessings of God, in order to be in right relationship to God in this world and to enjoy a future that would be blessed by God. That was their question. In the Orient, on the other hand, they did not ask that question. If they went looking for a master, they wanted to know how the hell you get out of here and bring an end to all this torment!

For example, Gautama grew up as a prince, with all the benefits of royal seclusion, the highest level of life possible in his time. When he was a relatively young man, he was taken on a trip through the streets where he saw the daily life of the people, who were sick and aging and suffering in all the ordinary, social, mortal ways. He did not see them as sinners who were suffering their turning away from God and who needed to be more positively associated with God in order to do better and feel better. He did not see them as the creations of the Deity, as his brothers and sisters under the one Divine. No—he was completely astonished by what he saw and he was, to his very depths, convinced that this is not a place in which to continue, that what life is about is not surviving and improving your circumstances and acquiring a positive moral character under God, or even a worldly life of success under God. That is not the business of life. The business of life, as Gautama realized it, is to find a way, through meditation, through understanding, through purification, and through release of desires, to escape completely from this condition of existence.

That disposition represented by Gautama, among others, that search for liberation, characterizes the classic traditions almost everywhere in the Orient. It is for the purpose of liberation that a person in the East seeks a teacher or becomes interested in a spiritual teaching. Spiritual teachings in the Orient are always associated with one or another ascetic disposition, the inversion of attention, the transcendence of this world. Inversion and transcendence are the fundamental principle, just as in Western religion the fundamental principle is that this world is to be interpreted positively as the creation of God, and therefore the problem of existence is a moral one.

Western religion comes out of the Middle East. The Middle East is the dividing line between the right-sided approach to life and the left-sided approach. The West has inherited Middle Eastern religion, but basically the path of the right side is not about religion at all. Western development is about life in the world, in which conditions of born existence are essentially considered to be just what they are—the conditions of born existence. Born existence is the game in which you are to survive and struggle, which you must take into account, and which your philosophy must reflect. The Middle East still has a religious or spiritual aura of a kind, but its principles, once they develop as Western history, as the right-sided history of mankind, do not appear in the form of religion. They appear in the form of our modern, technological, scientific society, which is essentially a-religious, not religious, a-spiritual, most often anti-religious and anti-spiritual. Thus, Western culture is basically oriented to manifest conditions and functions themselves.

Western people constantly confront the negative force of their own self-presumptions while trying to live a merely human, social, mortal life, advancing, succeeding, and surviving. Thus, Middle Eastern religion has provided psychological support for the right-sided man of the West. But, over time, the more involved Western men have become in the functions of manifest existence, in surviving and dealing with the material universe, and the more sophisticated human beings have become in their knowing, the less they have been able to justify the naive presumptions upon which this Western or Middle Eastern religion depends. Thus, more and more, people are being left with only sin. They do not even know what to call it anymore. They call it sin only if they see a God over against it. Basically they are left with an obsessed, negative, mortal life.

Having developed to this point, then, Westerners seeking after Truth are turning to the other side. They are hoping to be consoled by becoming Oriental, or left-sided. But once you have gone to the right, you can never go to the left and exclude the right side again. Thus, in this gesture toward the left side there is the possibility for consciousness as the whole body.

The Orient, on the other hand, which has been trying to transcend the gross conditions of worldly existence for centuries, has a very strong and sophisticated religious and spiritual tradition. But it also has the most dreadfully mortal social and human conditions on earth. Thus, people in the East today are reaching toward the right to find technological, scientific, social, cultural advantages within which to carry on their essentially negative philosophical point of view. But once you have gone so far to the left, you can never go all the way to the right and exclude the left side again, because you have already adapted to it. Thus, the East in its association with the West also has the possibility of becoming sensitive to the necessary or whole body point of view.

What we see in the world today are essentially the artifacts of the two sides in their independence, in their clashes with one another, in their distinctions. People today naively try to become associated with the ancient, classic systems of religion, spirituality, and philosophy, but they do not have the concentration for considering what these concepts are all about, what these motives in them are all about, what these belief systems and yogas are really all about. People today generally no longer represent the archetypal psychological dispositions that are at the root of all of these great enterprises, East and West. And unless those archetypal or psychological suppositions, presumptions, dispositions are actually true of you, you cannot fulfill them. Therefore, if you are truly moved to real or spiritual life, you have no choice but to inspect completely your own condition of existence.

You must begin to understand what the religious or spiritual life in Truth is really all about. You must be able to differentiate all your casually generated motivations that reflect old, conventional concepts, persuasions, and philosophies. You may have casually inherited your Western, Judeo-Christian mind without ever having been a very profound student of it. It just filtered in, through a little bit of churchgoing, a little bit of parental and social influence. But you must become responsible for the religious conventions you represent, through a very sophisticated investigation of Judeo-Christian thought and concepts, however casual your inheritance.

Although you are nominally associated with me, you are actually trying to fulfill your destiny as Jews and Christians and Moslems and Hindus and Buddhists and so forth. The mechanical aspects of our thought, feeling, and behavior are determined by even the most casual upbringing in those traditions. My Teaching Work has largely been with Westerners, and therefore it has always been associated with a very worldly level of drama. My Teaching Work does not look much like the way Oriental teachers deal with their devotees, because you all are not looking to be liberated. You have different problems altogether. You are sinful people! Being sinners is what you are up to.

True spiritual life turns out to be a different kind of thing altogether from what many people come to me for. Either they come to me for the left-sided reason, thinking of me as a yogic, ascetic teacher who is simply going to lead them inward and away from things, or they come thinking I am a sort of worldly philosopher who is going to provide them with a social life and amusing talks and a rather casual orientation toward changing themselves. Such people are always bothered by something. They are always on the verge of leaving, always on the verge of some great crisis and separation, always in some problem, always struggling. They have not heard the Teaching.

The Way of Radical Understanding or Divine Ignorance is the influence by which interested individuals, regardless of their disposition toward West or East, right or left, can make the necessary inspection of the totality of human existence. The essence of the Teaching of the Way of Radical Understanding is that God-Realization is the present Condition of existence, not in any sense the goal of existence that can be approached through efforts toward transcendence. Nor is the Divine in which we commune to be viewed simply as the Creator of this world, implying, therefore, a necessarily positive view toward the world and the functions of existence themselves. This Teaching is about present, radical, and continuous God-Communion as the very Condition and Truth of existence. The Divine is the Truth of existence, not just the Creator of the world. It is the Condition of all conditions, not just a great condition that creates all lesser conditions. And Divine Communion is not a matter of moving into a condition other than the present conditions, in order to escape them by exclusion through the inversion of attention.

Once you truly hear the Teaching, spiritual life becomes an essential responsibility, simple in principle. When you enjoy a positive orientation to the Teaching and to the Spiritual Master who communicates and demonstrates it—in other words, when you enjoy Divine Communion, then although the subjective artifacts of your past and your old disposition may appear, you have a sense of humor relative to them. Then not every day is a crisis. Subjective feelings come and go, and external circumstances tend to bother you somewhat, but there is no great moment. Literally nothing is threatened, once you are living in this Communion. Existence then becomes the creative process wherein you are living responsibly, purifying, changing, making things sacred, living the sacrifice that is real life. Then existence is not problematic. It is creative. It is a process of the confrontation of conditions, but it is humorous, already Enlightened. Nothing ultimate is at stake. It is just the game of the universe.

And there is nowhere to look for God. What is God is completely obvious under these conditions, even totally within the limits of your present perception. There is the Divine. It is not a matter of some other vision, some other experience, some inwardness. It is a matter of hearing, of being awakened from the sleep, the bondage, the problem, the dilemma by which you apprehend your present condition. In this hearing you are awakened to the Condition of this moment without all the concepts and contractions of energy and feeling.

When there is no obstruction to feeling-attention, then what is Divine, without qualification, is completely obvious. You need not create any strategy in your attention, to invert it or to exteriorize it, in order to find the Divine. Finding God is the illusion of the sinful individual, the one obsessed with suffering. Such people are always involved in programs of finding the Deity, finding someone to sustain them, because they are being themselves only, independent, separated, betrayed, unloved. You cannot find God in that case. Where God is completely obvious, God is nothing like what you think God must be. And to Realize God is nothing like what you imagine it must be.

You imagine that, since you do not Realize God, or do not feel completely Happy, sustained, and free under these ordinary conditions, then the Realization of God must be enjoyed under other kinds of conditions altogether. So you think that psychic awarenesses and visions are somehow the conditions under which God is Realized. But it is not true. Have those experiences, and there is no God then either, you see, unless you are converted in your feeling-attention even in that moment. In that moment of feeling-attention, then, you Realize God. But God-Realization has nothing whatever to do with those new conditions any more than with these old conditions. You become liberated from the search for conditions, attainments, goals as God-Realization, and you return to normal. Whatever conditions are to arise for you will arise for you, and you need not be the least bit concerned about them! You are finally free, in God-Realization, of the idiotic game of rising and falling with the conditions of existence.

Remain simply in that enjoyment at Infinity and forget about all the complications of the machinery of life and all your efforts to become Free, and be Happy. Be Happy and active as love in the world. As long as this world continues, you must perform action. You will necessarily perform action, because you are action. You are only action. So be converted in this God-Communion. Then your action is transformed. It fulfills the Law. It is a form of sacrifice, of love.

Be love and perform the actions of love until the universe disappears, and be willing to let it disappear. Be happy in any moment for it to disappear. Whatever satisfactions there are in the functional display in this moment cannot in any sense compare to the blissfulness of Divine absorption. Do not be strategically turned away from those satisfactions in the doubting that possesses the ego. Live as love in the form of all your relations. Living as love in God-Communion, rested at Infinity, you are not holding on to these relations any longer. You are just participating in them fully, openly, freely, Happily. You are not rejecting them, but neither are you clinging to them madly, out of fear. You are perfectly happy to have feeling-attention pass suddenly in this moment to Infinity, so that everything disappears.

There is nothing inherent in you that is holding you back from Infinity. Whatever you are holding on to is your position and therefore your destiny. Whatever you are holding back from Infinity, that is what you will continue to be. That is the destiny that will repeat itself in experience. If you are capable of being feeling-attention to Infinity, then conditions will arise for you, but they will also become obsolete and fall away.

The way to give up everything is not through strategic renunciation or turning in and up, but through love without qualification. Then everything falls away. Everything becomes God. Everything becomes enjoyable and not binding. When you can be released as love completely and fall into Infinity completely, then everything dissolves.

But you, you see, are afraid to dissolve. You think that you have to be in a position somehow, observing something, holding on to something, being held by something, whether it is in this gross form or in some subtle contemplation. You are afraid to feel, to release your consciousness to Infinity, because that means you will lose your point in space. You are going to lose your life—that is exactly true. Thus, only when the Happiness of Communion at Infinity becomes obvious to you will that dissolution be permitted to become perfect. Because it does involve the dissolution of everything, the dissolution of body, of all energy, all forms, all worlds, all that is mind, all concepts. It does involve that literally, you see. That is exactly what you are afraid will happen! (Laughter.) That is what you call death and try to prevent. And that is exactly what does happen in this Communion. Everything is given up, everything is dissolved at Infinity.

Infinity must become your pleasure. Then this world becomes humorous and livable. Then you can make something sacred out of it, without holding on to it. It will pass away. Everything passes away, everything is changing here. Everything is action. Everything you hold on to changes, because it is itself change. Therefore, holding on to a position obviously is not Truth. The surrender of all positions is true. Ultimately that becomes your position moment to moment, not just in intense moments of formal meditation, when you have temporarily relaxed from the games of life. Ultimately, there is no limitation under any conditions. Even while active and appearing in the ordinary way you are complete Zero, without a center, without any shapes whatsoever.

To the ordinary man that does not sound like Happiness—it sounds like some sort of craziness, some sort of tremendous, terrifying state, as Arjuna experienced in the *Bhagavad Gita* when he saw Krishna in his thousand-armed form. That is what that vision is all about—losing all ability to comprehend yourself in time and space. It is not just seeing somebody with a thousand arms. Actually, that would be wonderful and interesting. But to commune with Something with endless dimensions, to fall into Infinity yourself, is terrifying. When Arjuna was drifting into that open-ended Divine Condition, he shouted and screamed and told Krishna to please show him his two-armed, objective form, which was good enough! (Laughter.)

But my confession to you is that this Infinite existence is ultimate Bliss, the Great Happiness.

November 5, 1977

To See God as Reality

a talk by Da Free John

MASTER DA: Fundamentally the Adept is here to call people to Awaken, to enjoy insight into the karmic process. The Adept calls you to see the import of mind and how it is falsifying your presumption about your own Nature or Condition at this moment and causing you to be motivated through the mechanics of attention to the karmic possibilities of embodiment in this life and beyond. The fundamental Argument I bring to you is just this consideration of Awakening so that you will observe and understand the mechanics of manifest existence. The seed, the root, the fundamental process of manifest existence is this contraction that may be observed in the form of all kinds of physical, mental, and emotional associations, but ultimately it is discovered to be the fundamental force of the ego itself. It is a simple contraction or knot. When this is understood, then the necessity of manifest existence or karma is transcended.

Manifest existence is karmic existence. In that sense, manifest existence is negative, because it is made by a contraction from the infinite Bliss of Divine Existence. There is no ego without contraction from the Divine Condition. Ego is a contraction of the Divine Condition. This cosmos or universe is nothing but a contraction from the Divine State. If you can see it as such and awaken beyond that knot of self-contraction, then you will stand in the Divine State wherein there is no necessity for the cosmos or manifest form, because it is made only by limiting the Divine Condition. There is no need to limit the Divine Condition. There is no necessity to this manifestation. It arises mysteriously in the Divine, but the Divine is not simply in charge of it. It is built upon the

Divine, it is a pattern in the Divine, it is potential in the Divine. It need not be caused. It is mysteriously existing. But we can enjoy insight into the form of our participation in it so that we awaken to the Real or Divine Condition. If we will awaken to the Truth, then this world or manifest life is inherently transcended. We need not account for it in any complex, philosophical way if we will simply Awaken to the Truth, if we will simply observe the mechanics of our participation in karmic existence and Realize What is prior to it.

In that Condition, in the state of the Adept, it becomes clear how exactly the cosmos itself comes into being. The process of manifestation is tacitly obvious in the Awakened state: The appearing world is simply mind. It is nothing but mind, nothing at all but thought, nothing at all but a modification of Consciousness. This present moment is not a play of material forces in which Consciousness is somehow a secondary event. This moment is Consciousness. Mind is built upon Consciousness, and objects, elements, materiality, and cosmic form all precipitate from or in mind.

The simple Truth is that people do not realize that the universe is arising in Consciousness. They think that Consciousness is somehow inside themselves or inside the universe, that it is a small point of awareness within matter. They think the universe somehow stands in a great material space. They cannot account for the universe, they cannot account for themselves. They do not realize the seniority of Consciousness and the mechanical nature of mind, and they do not account for the universe on the basis of mind.

There are taboos against accounting for things in this way. These taboos are created by the karmic collective of humanity, which does not want attention to resort to its Root-Source or Condition, but rather wants to keep attention present in the mechanics of Nature so as to keep life in order and keep it reproducing itself. To support these taboos, God-ideas are created: "God is creating this world," "God is in charge of this world," "God wants us all to be born," "God wants us all to live," "God wants us to be limited or egoic beings, at least for now." All of these God-ideas are produced by the ego to account for egoic suffering.

The unillumined God-traditions conceive of God as Creator, but the high God-traditions conceive of God as Reality. Only those traditions that most directly emanate from the Adepts see God as Reality rather than merely as the Creator. To see God as Reality you must understand the karmic nature of manifestation and not make it so holy that it cannot be inspected and transcended. People are suffering from this holy egoity, in which the world is holy in its own right, in which Nature is holy, necessary, God-made, God-chosen. Therefore, such people are not Realizing God, and they are not moving beyond the lower stages of life.

February 12, 1982

What Is to Be Realized?

There is <u>only</u> the Radiant Transcendental Being, Who is One. All beings and things and worlds are ultimately and Really only Identical to That One, Who is God, the Divine Person.

Only God is Alive as everyone and everything. All beings and things and worlds are arising as spontaneous transformations or modifications of That One. God eternally Transcends the world and all beings, and yet the world and all beings are nothing but God. It is a Great and Passionate Mystery.

The individual being, manifest as the body-mind, is only a transformation or modification of the Radiant Transcendental Being or Divine Person. Wherever or whenever there is a psycho-physical being, the Radiant Transcendental Being is conscious as that limitation and feels Itself to be a particular being.

There is no internal self or soul within and independent of the body-mind. The individual body-mind is a modification or Play upon the Infinite, All-Pervading, Transcendental Being. The body-mind itself, in its contraction or recoil from the universal pattern of relations, suggests or implies the subjective internal self or independent soul idea. And once the body-mind or self pattern arises, it tends to persist, as a process of transformation, lifetime after lifetime, until there is Awakening to the Truth, or Translation into the Divine Domain—the Condition of Radiant Transcendental Bliss.

As the being adapts and evolves and achieves Ecstasy in the Divine, it Realizes its eternal inherence in That One and, ultimately, its Identity as That One. Such is Enlightenment, Liberation, or Salvation. Therefore, Enlightenment, Liberation, Salvation, or That which is to be Realized, is not a form of "status" or egoic achievement in this world, the after-death world, or the next lifetime, but it is the Condition of Love and Happiness, which transcends the body-mind, its experiences, its relations, and the world, even as the world continues.

The "being" that is Awakened to the Truth may abide simply as that Identity, excluding participation in the active pattern of the body-mind, its relations, and the world, and excluding as well the self-transcending gesture of Ecstasy in the Universal or Total Divine. Such is the disposition in the sixth stage of life. Just so, the being that is only beginning to understand its circumstance in God may embrace the lesser disposition of abiding in a state of simple absorption of self in the Radiance of the Transcendental Being. Such conditional Ecstasy characterizes fulfillment in the fourth and fifth stages of life, and it arises when the self or body-mind becomes contemplatively absorbed in the Divine Power that is experientially perceived by or within the body-mind itself. But in the Fullness of the seventh stage of life there is perfect, total, and most profound recognition that the total body-mind, all beings, and the total world of possibilities inhere in an eternal Condition of perfect Identity with the Radiant Transcendental Being. Then there is no reaction either toward inwardness or release of self through internal or external experience. The total body-mind and its conditions and relations are recognized to abide in inherent Identification with That One. Therefore, there is simple persistence as Transfigured Bliss or Love, whatever arises. Every moment of experience is Realized to be equally and totally Profound. This continues, through all the acts and moments and transformations of the body-mind in Love, until the body-mind and its experience are dissolved, passed away, or Outshined by the Radiant Transcendental Being.

The Living God, the Beloved of all beings, has, from eternity, become a Great Sacrifice. The Radiant One has become the process of all possibilities. We are not merely the creatures or victims of God, created and set apart to suffer for some inexplicable reason. We are the very Sacrifice of God. God is Alive as us. Our lives are the creative ordeal to which God is eternally submitted. We need only Realize the Living One and thus become capable of this Divine Sacrifice, which is an eternal creative ordeal of Love that leads, step by step, toward a Most Wonderful Transformation. Once we transcend the illusion of our dark separate selves and enter into the Divine Process, we see clearly that the existence and destiny of the world and every being is the Fullness of Love-Bliss in a perfectly Transformed state that has become One with the Person and the Domain of the Transcendental Divine.

This is my Testimony and my Confession. And it is the same Testimony and Confession proclaimed by all the Free Adepts who have appeared to serve mankind on Earth.

The Practice of Surrender Is a Ko-an

Introduction to Part II

A clenched fist, or an open hand. Master Da Free John has many times shown devotees these two "mudras" or bodily poses as signs of our fundamental options in any moment. Practice is to open the "fist" of the whole body-mind in every moment, and to keep it open.

Thus, the conception of the Way that Master Da Teaches is simple. But its execution is difficult. Once you actually locate the mechanism of practice, you can begin to establish a rhythm of understanding, surrender, and self-transcendence. But until then there is constant phasing and difficulty. To use Master Da's bodily analogy again, it is not enough to decide to open your fist. You have to locate the muscular gesture that will do the deed. And then you have to practice it.

One of the disheartening moments for many beginners comes when they suddenly recognize that they have almost no native talent for practice at all. To practice this Way requires, for most people, an arduous period of learning a completely new action rooted in consciousness that ultimately transforms every activity of mind and life. The learning takes time. It is frustrating and sometimes embarrassing. Occasionally you despair. But if you have "heard" the Teaching to any significant degree, then from the outset you know you have no choice but to go through the sacred ordeal.

The importance of hearing cannot be overemphasized. As long as we have egoic commitments—desires, plans, habits, schemes (karmas, in other words)—that have not been touched by the fire of Master Da's critical Argument, then our practice is always compromised and vitiated by those commitments. Master Da has spoken of "karmas below consciousness," or those seeds of egoic activity that have not yet become vulnerable to observation, insight, and radical understanding. He writes in *The Paradox of Instruction:*

> The foundation of this true spiritual Way is the hearing of this argument that is the essential Teaching. If you do not hear it, if you just take up the discipline and practices themselves in the hope of becoming Enlightened, or in the hope of becoming convinced of the argument itself as a result, you will remain, even in the midst of that discipline, still committed to the subjective principle, the flight from experience, the bird in the cage sense of "me" that is trying to escape, to be immune, like Narcissus. You will be obliged by that commitment even while you are trying to discipline yourself. And because the discipline is such a burdensome task under these conditions, it becomes very complicated. Out of that complication come the endless questions, the struggling within, the resistance, so that things as simple as lunch, or feeling, or service to others become very complex! All the problematic complication of this Way of spiritual life is just the failure to hear the argument, the failure to be most fundamentally convinced, the failure to be convicted and confessed in the whole being and so released into an orientation that is not the usual one, that is not the usual turning in upon the subjective root. (p. 61)

Part Two of this book presents Master Da's Teaching on the primacy of hearing and seeing, or intuitive self-understanding and emotional conversion to Spiritualized existence, respectively. In these essays and talks Master Da calls us to practice. He explains in detail the essence of all of the practical and meditative disciplines of the Way of Radical Understanding. That essence of practice is surrender to the

Divine Reality that has been, and is presently being, heard and seen by the devotee.

The secret of hearing, seeing, and the whole life of surrender is the Enlightening Grace Transmitted by the Spiritual Adept. Anyone who truly understands Master Da's arguments and instructions in this book will naturally begin to "find" or locate this "Baptism of Happiness." He or she will inevitably be drawn to practice the Way in Communion with Master Da as Divine Teacher, Presence, and very Being. The "answer" to the "ko-an" of surrender (how to "open your fist") is given by Grace. But it can only be received by those who have already begun to hear and see the Divine Spirit that breaks the shackles of doubt and opens us to infinite Being.

The Editors

Conversion to the Transcendental Way

Each of us inheres in Radiant Transcendental Being, the Bright or Divine Self, in Whom the Universe of all possibilities is arising as a great psycho-physical Process. But we are made superficial by attention to the Play of psycho-physical states, so that we abandon the intuitive position or disposition wherein our own Identity and the Condition of all conditions is obvious. Thus, we develop a state of presumed knowledge and conventional experience in which the physical or elemental world seems to be dominant, such that it appears to cause and also to be the final destiny of the conscious self and all that is mind.

In Truth, there is the Eternal Divine Self, and the total psycho-physical cosmos arises in It. But the conventional view (based on the superficial involvement of attention in phenomena) is that there is, first of all, the physical-elemental world, and mental states as well as conscious being merely arise as individual and temporary effects of that world.

The obvious pettiness and fruitless absurdity that seem to characterize much or even most of our human life are simply an expression of our superficiality. Such qualities are not necessary, but they are inevitable until we enter into the profound disposition of Transcendental understanding. Our superficial existence is characterized by a seemingly endless play of mutually contradictory doubts and beliefs, facts and opinions relative to ourselves and the world. Therefore, our science and our religion also tend to be superficial, and equally so, since they are equally based on the identification of existence with the superficial phenomenal observability of the world and the body-mind.

Our existence is a trial whereby we are gradually or quickly converted from superficiality to profundity. Ultimately, we learn to trust and identify with the Divine Self or Radiant Transcendental Being, in Whom the world and the body-mind-self are arising. That One is latent with all possibilities and is prior to or greater than that fraction of possibility that presently appears (or is presently noticed). Thus, It is greater than the world, the body, or the conscious mind. We must love, trust, and surrender into the Condition and Identity of the manifest self and world, Who is not merely Unconscious (or "the" Unconscious) or a negative Void, but Who is Realized as the Radiant Fullness of Love-Bliss, beyond the limiting power of conventional knowledge and experience.

The argument or consideration that I present to you is founded on the Realization of the Truth, and it draws the hearer into the prior position or disposition of intuitive Identification with the Radiant Transcendental Being. When this conversion is total, apparent human existence is in the seventh or ultimate stage. In that stage of life, the conventions of egoic individuality and all superficial views relative to the status of the world, of mind, and of conscious being are transcended. Thus, existence in human form becomes a transparent and spontaneous expression of Radiant Transcendental Being. And, more and more, the various motions or aspects of the manifest self or body-mind relax into the Transcendental Radiance, Love-Bliss, and Peace of the Divine Self, so that the individual appears more and more to bear the characteristics of renunciation, desirelessness, or freedom from the binding or Happiness-frustrating power of all the apparent aspects of psycho-physical embodiment.

The argument or consideration whereby this conversion or Realization is served may be stated in a relatively simple form.

First, we must "hear" or understand that our lives are

commonly devoted to the pattern of Narcissus, which is the avoidance of relationship, or systematic and total psycho-physical self-contraction.

Second, we must "see" the Truth, or be converted from the disposition of self-contraction to that of ecstasy, or self-transcendence. This is a matter of the total conversion of the psycho-physical self, via the full conversion of our feeling-attention, to the Radiant Transcendental Being. Such conversion is expressed in a number of ways, depending on the stage of life and the unique characteristics of the individual, but it is fundamentally a matter of conversion, or a turn about, from the conventions of presumption (or knowledge) and experience that characterize the superficial or unillumined ego. Thus, it is primarily a matter of awakening to the disposition of ultimate or Transcendental Ignorance, in which the conventional force of all arising states of knowledge or experience is transcended in the Realization of Mystery, or the Realization that, no matter what arises, "I" do not know what it is.

The third and final aspect of this consideration, or conversion to Truth, is practice. Practice that is founded on the understanding and conversion I have just described is not truly a means toward ultimate Realization but a more and more profound expression of Realization, or prior Happiness.

Those who "hear" and "see" most immediately and profoundly enter more quickly and directly into the seventh stage of life (and they likewise quickly develop the free renunciate qualities in the seventh stage of life[1]). Others may

---

1. Renunciation, in the Way of Radical Understanding, is intuitive and active abandonment of the ego as the operating principle of human life. Such renunciation therefore does not involve any strategic or ego-based change of behavior in the conventional renunciate style of ascetical self-denial. Practitioners of this Way certainly simplify and harmonize their daily lives,

make a slower transition to the seventh stage and the free renunciate qualities (which simply express the ecstasy of inherence in Radiant Transcendental Being, transcending psycho-physical states of knowledge and experience). In any case, it is the same understanding and Realization that Embraces all who become established in the Way that I Teach.

December 30, 1981

engaging all action as God-Communion, but they do not in principle abandon natural human relations or activities (spouse, family, sexuality, etc.).

However, as Realization matures in the seventh or Enlightened stage of life, even the Awakened motives toward benign physical and psychic activity in the manifest realms dissolve in the Sufficiency of Divine Self-Abiding. The "free renunciate qualities" that develop in this stage include a simplified lifestyle (which may appear even extremely ascetical), a natural preference for peaceful solitude and personal inactivity, and an obvious Indifference to the superficial play of relations. The root of these and similar qualities, as Master Da indicates in this essay, is true ecstasy, or perfect Identity with the Self of all beings and the "Love-Bliss" that is the Substance of all phenomena.

The Adept Is the Remover of Doubt

by Frans Bakker, M.D.

T*he following account demonstrates how "hearing" Master Da's Teaching and "seeing" the Divine Presence in his Company lead naturally to practice of the Way of Radical Understanding. It shows how the Adept both Awakens and continually (and very humorously) tests the Realization and practice of devotees.*

Frans Bakker's story is also useful because he, like so many other devotees, endured a long period of futile attempts to practice the disciplines of the Way (relative to work, food, sexuality, service, meditation, etc.) before becoming fully established in the foundation principles of hearing and seeing. Testimonies like Frans's, then, stand as vivid reminders of both the pitfalls of bypassing the foundations of practice and the virtues of engaging those foundations, each in its appropriate moment in the process.

Frans Bakker is a member of The Advaitayana Buddhist Order of The Johannine Daist Communion,[1] and a lecturer and educator for The Laughing Man Institute.

I was brought up by my parents in Holland with minimal exposure to religion or a notion of God. I was, of course, influenced by the Christian tradition all around me. I clearly

1. The Johannine Daist Communion is the spiritual fellowship of practitioners of the Way Taught by Master Da Free John. See "About The Johannine Daist Communion," p. 143, for an explanation of the name of the Communion and a description of its four divisions.

remember a kind of fascination with the person of Jesus. This was the most concrete feeling relative to God that touched me.

Often I was sadly aware, however, that Jesus was long dead. I used to fantasize what it would have been like to live in his time and Company. I felt that perhaps that would have made a difference, because I did not exactly see anyone around me *living* a God-life. When I grew up beyond my more "romantic" inclinations as an adolescent, I became a medical student. The idealistic influences of Bible, Sunday School, and the figure of Jesus faded away, making place for the scientific mood of realism and doubt. Although I was profoundly influenced by all that and became more and more "heady" and realistic, dealing with the human body in all its mortal aspects, I never completely lost a sense of awe and wonder about the Mystery of it all.

This sense that life had to be more than what it seemed on the surface finally led to my contact with Master Da Free John. He not only confirmed my intuition that there was more to me and the world around me than "met the eye." He obviously lived a life that was built on an entirely different assumption and Realization. Here was a mysteriously free and unconventional being. I remember first reading his books and then seeing him for the first time: My heart leaped up for joy. If he was free, I was free, utterly, priorly free in God. There *was* God, and this real God was entirely different from the God of my early religious background. It was possible to realize God, to *be* God, radiantly Happy and Free. This intuition was awakened in me from the very beginning when I first set eyes on Master Da's Teaching and Person. I remember the happiness I felt to see how my childhood fantasy had come true. I could actually live with a Realized Being!

And so I did. On the basis of this feeling-intuition I moved from Holland to America and entered into a different Way of life in Master Da's spiritual community. Many times I forgot the fundamental Vision or intuition of God. Having lost the Vision, I often became a seeker trying to find it again, and meanwhile struggling with the disciplines of the Way of Understanding taught by Master Da. The old mood of doubt crept in slowly, but strongly. Being a doctor did not make it easier because of the adolescent, secular materialism that is at the root of modern medicine.

Sometimes the God-Vision was restored and the Way seemed possible again. It took incredible commitment on the part of Master Da Free John, relentless sacrifice and service, to invoke the Truth in me and others constantly and to "interfere" with our mechanisms of doubt, apathy, complacency, mediocrity, etc.

At one point over a year ago (after I had been here more than five years), in meditation I suddenly became clearly aware of the Truth again. Not only that, I knew that Da Free John was absolutely serious about this matter of God-Realization. He meant for it *actually* to happen in *my* case. This insight startled and amazed me. I saw in a flash that after my first awakening I had basically despaired of this possibility, becoming an egoic seeker of experience, even of the ultimate Experience down the line. But now God was tangibly obvious again.

Did I really want this dissolution of self? It scared me. Yet, I also knew there was no alternative. For the first time I was fully awakened to the fact that "I" was part of a greater process. What was to happen had nothing to do, ultimately, with what "I" wanted or not. It was at that point that I relaxed. I heard the Teaching and I saw the Vision of God again, and much more fully than before. There was much more of a mood of spontaneous surrender into this remarkable

Process that is life, God, Radiant Being. Practice became inevitable, and much more happy.

In September 1982, I was initiated into The Advaitayana Buddhist Order of The Johannine Daist Communion. Master Da's spiritual Influence in my life became more and more magnified. I felt more and more clearly his Transmission, his testing, and his interference with the mechanisms of my avoidance of Life. I saw how the Spiritual Master's Presence was reflected in everything around me, inviting natural self-observation and surrender.

In Master Da's personal Company this process was enhanced tremendously. I was invited to his hermitage retreat several months ago. Everything at that place seemed to breathe and radiate the Master-Presence. I felt on fire. I practiced conscious surrender continually. My tendencies as a conventional being became increasingly obvious, constantly rubbed up against the edge of Freedom. Master Da Free John was revealed to me as a great manifestation of the very Divine, one who is madly confessed in and as that One. Many times I was moved to tears of joy seeing this vision of the Spiritual Master's Divinity. And many times I felt utterly liberated in God myself by the Grace of his Transmission.

At the same time that he was radiating this Enlightening Grace, Master Da was also spontaneously interfering with the Narcissism of all those around him, constantly testing our stability in the God-Vision. He sometimes looked to me like a Divine boxer—dancing ecstatically through the ring, giving effective "jabs" right and left, and then coming in full weight to floor you, and all the time showing that he was just pointing to tendencies that have force only when you identify with them.

On one particular night, having received a number of those jabs myself and Master Da's several criticisms of the practice of all devotees, I was starting to feel "groggy." Many of the criticisms, I could see, were true of me. At this point Master Da swung fully around to me and asked if I were *really* practicing at the level of responsibility that I claimed. I hesitated for a moment and said, "I think so, Master."

"You *think* so!" he exclaimed. "Well, it seems to me that this is the best sign that you are obviously not practicing the Way as a member of The Advaitayana Buddhist Order. If you have to *think* about it, how can it be true?"

Master Da continued to criticize and berate me for several minutes along these lines. It was one of those testing moments. I felt weakness in my knees, as if I were even physically about to collapse into the old mood of doubt and to identify with what human flesh is heir to. But in that moment I saw it was not necessary. I observed what I was tending to do, relaxed, and felt into the Spiritual Presence of the Adept—which was obvious even as he was criticizing me face to face. I regenerated my practice in that moment, surrendering into his Spiritual Company. Then he asked me simple and yet profound questions:

"Frans, do you love God?"

I said yes.

"Do you love your Spiritual Master?"

I said yes again. I did not merely say it. My entire being responded to these questions with a wholehearted "yes," completely vanishing the mood of doubt and seeing again that there is God and that God is sufficient, God is our prior Condition, our "heart's desire." And that was the end of my "interview" that day by the Spiritual Master.

Master Da Free John is the Agent of the Great One, the living Divine. He always points us to that One and thereby liberates us from the mood of doubt.

The Practice of Surrender
Is a Ko-an

a talk by Da Free John

The Teaching of Master Da Free John is an expression of his direct, face-to-face response to those who have come to him for spiritual guidance and Blessing. Thus, as in the discourse below, his talks and essays are frequently addressed to those who are already practicing or attempting to practice the Way that he exemplifies and Teaches.

This talk was given at Land Bridge Pavilion, an open-air Communion Hall at The Mountain of Attention Sanctuary in northern California. It was addressed to a large gathering of practitioners who were just then learning the basic devotional disciplines of prayerful surrender to the Divine that Master Da offers to all beginners.

DEVOTEE: Master, my question is—I don't know how to put it exactly, but, I don't know how to use your Glance when you look at me in the Communion Hall or at any time.

MASTER DA (humorously): Get out of the way! (Great laughter.)

DEVOTEE: When I'm looking at you my eyes often go out of focus and I find myself drifting. I feel as though I should be conscious, whatever that means, and I feel as though I should do something. And I find that is also the case in my daily life—I always think there is something I should be doing.

MASTER DA: Surrendering is what you should be doing.

DEVOTEE: I don't know how to do that.

MASTER DA: Right. (He laughs.) Until you can surrender naturally and spontaneously, the matter of surrender is a great problem. Before you became associated with me you did not surrender, but you had a lot of problems. Now you have become associated with me and surrender has become one of your problems! (Laughter.)

My first human teacher, Rudi,[1] used to have this problem. Now I loved Rudi dearly, but I also learned a very fundamental lesson about surrender by practicing in his company and observing him. For Rudi the whole problem of life was how to surrender. He surrendered like a man lifting a two-thousand-pound weight! Surrender for him was a great effort, a great physical effort. He would talk about it—you have even heard me using his expression "tearing your guts out." He would make a gesture like this (Master Da pretends to cut himself with a knife) as if he were committing hara-kiri. Surrender was not natural to Rudi. It was obvious to him that surrender was the Truth and the Way of God-Realization. On the other hand, it was also obvious to him that he was a man full of tendencies, desires, and self-possession, and that, in fact, so was everyone.

Thus, there is Narcissus, and there is the truth that he must surrender. That is true. And you are you, and the truth is that you must surrender. But how to get from Narcissus to surrender (laughter)—that is the problem. Rudi's method

1. Rudi (Albert Rudolph) was Master Da Free John's spiritual Teacher from 1964–68. He helped Master Da prepare the foundation for the mature phases of his spiritual life. (Rudi, also called Swami Rudrananda, died February 21, 1973.) For an account of Master Da's years with Rudi, see *The Knee of Listening* by Da Free John.

was a very muscular one, and at an early stage of your practice surrender does have a kind of muscular quality. You must simply do it. It is true, you have to tear your guts out until surrender becomes quite natural, quite spontaneous, or at least begins to become somewhat subtler as an effort. You want to surrender like an Enlightened woman, and instead you have to surrender like a woman in trouble! This means that your surrendering has to be more obvious, more emotional, more physical, more in the form of service, and not complicated by subjective puzzling over it. Do it as best you can, completely, constantly, in spite of the fact that you are frustrated, and in spite of the fact that surrender is not profound at times. Give yourself up. If I look at you or you look at me and then you give yourself up, and there is still great tonnage of you left over (great laughter), this cannot be helped, you see. The fact that you cannot surrender totally, spontaneously, directly, fully, altogether, crown to toe and toe to crown from the heart, is part of the purifying process of your practice. Obviously, you cannot do that. If you could surrender so perfectly, to deal with you all would not take so much work on my part.

Surrender is a living process because you are a being adapted to doing something quite other than surrendering. You are a being adapted to a self-possessed way of existing. Every time you gain a little more familiarity with your possibilities, you simply gain more structures to manipulate for self-fulfillment. Even in your spiritual practice, as soon as you become familiar with higher or subtler structures of this body-mind with which you perhaps have previously had no familiarity, you will tend to use them as more of this armor, more of the self-game of Narcissus.

It is only in hearing the Truth that you surrender. It is only in the moment when you see me as Spirit-Presence that you surrender to me. In other words, it is only in the moment of the Awakening of intuition and the spontaneous regeneration of the heart that surrender is natural, simple, direct, true. In all other moments, we practice from the point of view of that intuition, it is tacitly present, but at the same time it is covered over by all of the structures of the body-mind. Therefore, our discipline must be deliberate. Our discipline is hot. It produces friction because we resist it even the very moment we do it. And we must do it because, having "heard" the Truth, having "seen" the Spiritual Master and the Divine Reality, we know this surrender to be the Way. On the other hand, all the structures of this body-mind resist doing such a thing. Therefore, to do it in the moment when we resist it also produces heat, "tapas," [2] purifying fire.

The endless complaint of devotees is that they cannot do it or they do not do it perfectly or they are not good devotees. Devotees are always complaining that to live the practice hurts. It does not flatter you, you see, because every moment you practice you are made even more familiar with your resistance to practice. That is the way it is. That is part of the physics that enables practice to be fruitful. It is that aspect of the physics of this practice that enables you to see the difference between God-Realization and states of the body-mind.

Though it moves by stages, this practice is not properly understood as progressive experience, so that when you enter into the seventh stage of life you represent a big experience or a great deal of experience, gross and subtle and all the rest. The significance of the stages of this Way is not that we accumulate experience. The significance of the stages is that

2. Tapas means austerity, the "heat" or "fire" of spiritual discipline. Traditionally, tapas is engaged through intentional, forced asceticism and motivated disciplines of self-denial. In the Way of Radical Understanding, the primary source of tapas is the demand for active love (service) and radical understanding, and the "heat" of practice is a form of "natural asceticism."

we transcend experience, and in the seventh stage we have
transcended <u>all</u> experience. In some secondary sense experience has also been there but it has been transcended in the
process. That is the key to this Way of life. The Way is
founded in hearing and seeing, it is founded in the Truth, the
intuition of the Heart.[3] All practices in this Way are generated
on the basis of that hearing, that heartfelt response. Therefore,
each stage of experience is transcended by that intuition. In
this Way we examine, inspect, and become responsible for all
of the functions of ordinary life. Likewise, we become familiar
with and responsible for the higher structural functions, the
subtler or mystical dimensions of awareness. But all of these
phenomena are transcended in the process through intuition.

In the intuition of God our surrender is inevitable. It is
spontaneous in that moment. Thus, if you approach me
recoiled upon yourself and you look at me or I look at you, you
are made to feel yourself more profoundly. You enter into
that doubt which is self-possession. This fearful doubting is
the very mood of self-possession. Part of my function is to
awaken you to the actual nature of your present approach.
You are constantly made to confront this limitation, this
essentially self-possessed state of life and even of approach to

---

3. The "Heart" is another name for the Divine Self, the Intuition or
Realization of the Radiant Transcendental Being or God. The origin of the
term is the experiential association of the Awakening to the Self-Nature with
the sense of the opening of the heart-root in the right side of the chest, and
the sense of the mind or process of thought and attention falling into its root
or origin in that "locus" associated with the trunk of the body. However,
Master Da capitalizes this term to distinguish the Transcendental Divine
Nature from the three aspects of the psycho-physical heart of the body-mind:
the physical organ, whose epitome is on the left side of the chest; the psychic,
feeling subtle center in the middle of the chest; and the heart-root or
functional seat of the essential self on the right side of the chest.

In this talk Master Da frequently uses the term "heart" (with a lower
case "h") to refer to the actual, bodily heart as the epitome of the whole body-
mind and the seat of conscious being.

me—and you continue to study the Teaching, you continue to practice its disciplines, and you continue to surrender. In moments the heart is clarified. In moments it feels as if the barriers have been dissolved. In moments one's experience is transformed. Sometimes surrender is made more difficult, at other times more glamorous.

But ultimately, in the paradoxes of this meeting, the heart is unburdened. It is relieved of its associations with this body-mind. First it is relieved of its associations with the lower, grosser realm, the realm of the lower coil, the realm of the navel, the body in its desiring, its sexuality, its eating and tussling with others, its acquisitions, its willfulness, its thinking, the extended nervous system in its orientation to the gross dimension. Then at another stage we are purified of the core of the body-mind, the subtler dimension, including those higher aspects of the mind that mystics commonly claim to be the domain of God. What is perceived in mystical contemplation is essentially phenomena of the brain that are covered up or are not functioning in the ordinary waking state.

Thus, we must be purified in our physical life, our emotional life, our sexual life, our mental life, our psychic life, and our higher intuitive life. In this Way of practice, in the fifth stage of life you look up and you see the subtle lights and you hear the mind saying, "This is God, this is heaven," but you will realize in that moment too that you are not surrendering. Soon you will pass beyond all of that. The higher mind will break up and you will go beyond the states of mind and be given some rest for a moment in which to realize that you are looking into the mindless void. You are not surrendering. Popular mysticism goes to the brain-mind and is satisfied with either the subtle visions, sounds, and objects or a certain quiescence, but we must go to the heart.

Just as every stage of this practice must be generated from the heart on the basis of hearing and seeing, the feeling response, so, ultimately, all the limits of the heart itself must be penetrated, because whatever is in the navel and whatever is in the brain are all in the heart. They all have their seat in the heart. Thus, until the heart itself is penetrated in the sixth stage and beyond, we are still not surrendering. At each stage of the inspection of the phenomena of experience we are confronted with our self, our Narcissism, our failure to surrender. And we are obliged to persist in each stage until the crisis of the penetration of that particular limit is passed.

Ultimately, we must penetrate this heart itself. We must go to the "atom." Ultimately, it is the practice of God-Communion at the heart that must occupy us. The atom, the illusion of separate existence, the root of the person or the ego-soul, must itself be overcome after all of its experiences or emanations have been inspected and released in the earlier stages. Even this sixth stage of life must be transcended, you see. Merely to resist this separate existence is not auspicious, it is not God-Realizing.

In the seventh stage we realize there is no one to surrender—that what was previously struggled with was not something other than our own ordinariness struggling with itself. All the limitations, all the difficulties of practice, in other words, are like one hand wrestling with itself and always somehow finding an opponent. (Laughter.) It was an illusory match! In the seventh stage there is no one to surrender. All the failures of surrender have been understood and the limit on the heart is broken. That limit no longer exists. The involuntary contraction of this body-mind has ceased and quite naturally does not recur.

Therefore, we have not truly surrendered until we have ceased to be the body-mind, until the body-mind has ceased to have power to define Consciousness, to define Energy, to define Love, to define Life, to define Existence.

This practice, then, is a kind of "ko-an," a kind of

humorous problem, a puzzle, a dilemma. But we are Awakened from the heart through hearing and seeing from the beginning. That hearing and seeing is the principle of our practice. And we must simply practice, you see. Even at the very beginning when we see how awkward we are, how unfeeling we are, we must live the practice, live the disciplines, oblige the body-mind to readapt, and surrender the body-mind in this Divine Company. Simply surrender to the Spirit-Power, allow It to show Itself. Do not be so busy falling back on yourself to see how it is going. Simply give yourself up to me in my Spiritual Form. At times it is difficult, and there are other times when it is not difficult.

That is the way it is, you see. Devotees complain about the Way as if they were uniquely failing at this affair and as if they were not getting superior Help (laughter), but that simply is the way it is. That is the way it has always been, and that is the way it always will be. Spiritual practice is a difficult process for many, many reasons. Your prior adaptation, your identification with the body-mind itself, your unevolved state—all of these factors make it difficult. There is a living structure that is here to be transformed, and it has other business that occupies its attention.

The Principle that makes it all humorous, possible, and ultimately fruitful is in this hearing, this Communion. The relationship to the Spiritual Master is the Principle that makes the practice fruitful. It is also the Principle with which you are at war. The individual does not want to surrender by tendency. The individual will surrender only on the basis of intuition or hearing. If you consult the body-mind itself, it only wants to be involved with itself. It would like to occupy itself with techniques, it would like to improve itself, it would like to have better experience. It would like to feel good, it would like to be immortal. It would like to be already Enlightened. It would like to be superior to all beings. It would like to be Guru. (Laughter.) Spiritual Master! Everybody wants to be a Spiritual Master. People have not the slightest idea what that function involves.

Narcissus, you see, is literally at war with his own Help. You observe this war in your relationship with me. That is also the way it is. That is also something that devotees have always complained about—this evil in themselves which is at war with everything true and is ultimately at war with the Spiritual Master and the Divine in every moment. But it is not absolutely or only true that you are at war with me (though that certainly is the case!). It is simply that the body-mind, by virtue of its tendencies, is reluctant. In every moment when you fall out of sympathy with me, fall out of this hearing, this seeing, this relationship with me, you fall into the structures of the body-mind itself. You see how knotted up it is. Thus, you must persist in your surrendering.

Bring yourself to the study of the Teaching. Submit yourself to the text, submit yourself to the Word of the Spiritual Master. Engage in the personal, moral, and devotional practices of the Way, bodily and with all of your feeling. Engage in devotion not only on the formal occasions of sitting meditation in the morning and in the evening, but in some form or another engage in devotional surrender all day long—because you have heard, because the heart is Awake to me.[4]

---

4. In this talk Master Da is addressing devotees in The Free Communion Church. Such practitioners are actively engaged in practicing the initial personal, moral, and devotional disciplines of the Way that he Teaches. His admonition to surrender via these practices also applies to devotees in the more advanced orders of The Johannine Daist Communion, who learn and develop more technical versions of these disciplines.

   Other readers, including beginning students in The Laughing Man Institute, should simply allow the disposition of surrender to be awakened in them through study or "listening" to Master Da's Teaching to the point of "hearing."

Everything in you that is other than that awakened heart is what makes your practice a dynamic process. It means that there will be times when you feel "out of it," overwhelmed by your negativity and your symptoms. You must have more humor about all of that. You must see it arise enough so that it has no more significance to you than a headache, one that is expressed in psychological terms. Then that negativity is just something you live with. It does not animate you particularly. It is just that the tendency persists. And that is all it is: a tendency, a setup in the nervous system and in the endocrine system at the moment. It is a setup in the bloodstream and in the way the wave patterns are working in the brain at that moment. The heart is not bound by that. It observes all of that. It sees what a cranky animal the psycho-physical person is and has some humor about it.

Particularly in those moments you must learn to practice with great intensity. You must surrender more profoundly with a tacit recollection of your understanding of the true nature of your feeling in relation to me. And you must learn in this process, you see, to make use of me, to make use of my Spiritual Blessing-Transmission. You must learn how more and more profoundly to make use of me.

DEVOTEE: Master, that making more use of you comes from intuition and studying the Teaching. Is that right?

MASTER DA: Right. And surrender! (Laughter.) To hear the Teaching means that you hear me, because the Teaching did not fall out of the sky. I have communicated this Teaching! And if you hear me, then you can live with me in Spiritual terms. You cannot just hear the Teaching, you see, and go off to be alone with it. To hear the Teaching means to be established in a relationship with me. Therefore, having heard, you must see me, you must live with me, you must practice in my Company. That is the secret of this Way of Life—not to be self-involved, not just to have a mental understanding, but to live with me directly. The more you do that, the more you fulfill the discipline, then also the more the limits, tendencies, and programs of Narcissistic structures break up, loosen, and give the heart room in which to transcend the body-mind.

This intuition, this hearing and seeing, is the seed of the Divine process. But it does not show all of its signs in this Transfigured[5] body-mind until spiritual maturity. Having matured to the point of the seventh stage of life, we essentially rest in the same intuition that was present in the first moment of hearing. On the other hand, the body-mind stands in a totally different relationship to that Truth. Having passed through all of the stages into the seventh stage on the basis of the principle of the Heart, in Communion with the Spiritual Master, the body-mind itself is changed. It is literally Transfigured by the Radiance intuited at the heart. It is pervaded by the Divine Radiance, not just by the material forces or the energies coursing through the nervous system, but by the Transcendental Radiance that is the same as Consciousness.

Thus, whatever purifications, modifications, awakenings, and kinds of growth and experience must occur before you

5. "Transfiguration," "Transformation," and "Translation" are technical terms that describe the unfolding process of God-Realization in the seventh stage of life. Transfiguration is the pervasion of body and mind by Transcendental Radiance or Light. Bodily and mental Transformation involves the arising of supernormal signs or abilities, such as healing, power, longevity, and psychic capabilities. Divine Translation is the ultimate evidence of God-Realization, wherein the limited psycho-physical body, mind, and world are no longer noticed—not because the consciousness has withdrawn from all such phenomena, but because it has entered into such profound absorptive Realization of the Divine Condition that all phenomena are, as Master Da Confesses, "Outshined" by that Light. Please see especially chapter 7 of *The Enlightenment of the Whole Body* by Da Free John.

will be perfectly submitted to the Heart will appear as time goes on. In the beginning, this surrendering is, in general, more difficult, more associated with vital problems and lower psychological difficulties. How could it be otherwise? That is how you have lived. What did you expect? All of a sudden you want to be a yogi-princess? (Laughter.) It cannot happen. Maybe a couple of moments here and there just to make you feel better (laughter), but spiritual life is Holy War.[6] And the great warriors are people who are awake to the Leader, awake to the Master. They are given up to the Truth, they are full of their purpose, and they are not weakened by their associations. So, do not be concerned about your reactions, your still mediocre state. Just continue to surrender. Continue to live the practice as it is given. Continue to submit to the Word of the Teaching, and to the devotional disciplines. This is the best thing to do most diligently in the beginnings of this practice.

In the years when I was living with Rudi I could feel heat all over my body all the time. I felt as if I were burning up all the time from the intense frustration of the practice. I was burning up all the time, and that burning up eventually purified this mechanism. In other words, it made it responsive to the Heart, made it kneel to the Truth, so that it could be lived in a natural way and not be a mechanism for accumulating urgent, deluded demands that prevented the natural state. After a period of time this lower coil of the body-mind began to become more easeful, more natural, more happy, and the higher structures of the body-mind quite naturally became the field of my practice. So it is with you. In some cases there are more of the yogic phenomena, perhaps. Even some kinds of superficial mystical experience may arise at the beginning of

6. Master Da Free John uses the term "Holy War" in the most benign and truly spiritual sense. It signifies the commitment to active, bodily transformation of life and human relations that characterizes genuine spiritual practice.

practice, at least in some cases. But what is really going on in the beginning of this practice is the purification and harmonization of this ordinary, lower person and his bodily, emotionally reactive, and mentalizing character. If there is any yoga occurring, it is basically a yoga that purifies that lower being.

Therefore, just live the life of service, the life of love, the life of your ordinary obligation from day to day. Live your <u>surrender</u> simply, personally, through your right action, through your feeling, through your study.

In time practice becomes in some sense less of a muscular affair, because you become purified and harmonized by the discipline and by the Grace that enters into your life through the doorway of the discipline. You see how difficult a process it is. That is part of the suffering of life to be observed. Why should you want to have to go through such a thing again? Existence itself will always be difficult until you have transcended experience and all the structures to which you are adapted in your desire and your mind. It is not only calamities in Nature and in the human world that make life suffering. This psycho-physical structure itself is suffering, and we are simply bound up in it. We have all of its adventure to go through.

So let it be immensely difficult only this one time. Enter into the God-Realm in this lifetime. Why not do it that way? Enter into the Divine Destiny. Enter into the Bliss of God. You could do everything else. In some sense you will do everything else anyway, but in a more Lawful form than the downtown man, than Narcissus. But devote your life to the Truth and live out this Holy War. Do not be like the usual man, who turns this lifetime into something that simply serves another lifetime, who does nothing more than what is necessary to make him do the same thing all over again.

October 28, 1978

A Demonstration of the Simplicity of Practice

by Canada Sheinfeld

T*he relationship to the Spiritual Master is the all-encompassing, single Condition of existence for those who practice the Way of Radical Understanding. The Master-Presence, once truly contacted or entered into, works to purify, balance, and Awaken the being at all times, and under all conditions. The great marvel of this relationship is that it is completely untouched by changes of time, space, and person.*

The following is an example of a vivid dream wherein a devotee received instruction in her practice of surrender along the lines Master Da outlined in the preceding talk. Canada Sheinfeld is a practitioner in The Free Communion Church, which is the sacred gathering of "maturing beginners" in The Johannine Daist Communion.

I had the following dream in January 1983. At this time Master Da was living away from the general culture of devotees in a secluded retreat. I had begun to perceive a certain level of unnecessary complication in my practice and a need to embrace the simplicity of the Way. This dream was a clear and simple expression to me of the primacy of surrender to the Spiritual Master in the face of all that may arise in this mysterious process in his Company.

In the dream, many devotees were informally gathered with Master Da. He circulated among us, freely granting his Darshan (the blessing of viewing the Enlightened one). Then the time came when the Master was to sit formally in meditative Communion with everyone. I was among the first to enter the room and I found a space to sit at the front, close to Master Da's seat. As he entered, I could feel the magnification of his Presence, and my entire body, mind, feeling, and attention were suddenly given to him. There was nothing but that Infinity of his Presence. I rested deeply in that Happiness.

Master Da began to talk. As he did so, an incredible array of "stuff" began to arise and move out of me. I practiced this simple devotion of feeling and attention to the Master and, as I did this, more and more of this psychic stuff was arising and moving through me with greater force. I could not identify what it all was or where it was coming from. It felt like an exorcism or a massive purification that exceeded all of my comprehension of myself. It was as if I were being purified of lifetimes.

At one point Master Da reached across the small table in front of him and took my hand. Throughout his talk he fondled and touched it, continuously gracing me with a tacit and compassionate gesture of his love and constant attention to devotees. I continued to practice with a great will, abiding in the Master's Company, feeling how the whole practice is simply that abidance and how I need not be distracted from him, from the absolute Pleasure of his Presence. Meanwhile the purification was continuing, and bizarre sounds, spontaneous bodily movements, weeping, etc., were spewing out of me as Master Da continued to speak.

This practice of inhering in the Master's Company and enduring the intense purification continued for a long time until eventually I awoke from the noises I was making. I lay awake for an hour or so continuing in this simplicity of practice. I felt both worked over, devastated, and purged bodily *and* extremely grateful for this Blessing of Master Da's Presence and this simple demonstration of the practice. I could see that the discipline is simply this devotion of feeling and attention to the Spiritual Master, and that everything arising in me and my experience is secondary and not the point.

What Master Da writes is true: "There is no Friend greater than the [Spiritual] Master." [1] The relationship to him is the salvation, the bridge beyond ourselves to Inherence in the Happiness of our native State. I offer praise to Master Da Free John. We are blessed by his Appearance in our midst!

---

1. Da Free John, *The Hymn of the Master* (The Dawn Horse Press, 1982), verse 44.

Yield to God

a talk by Da Free John

MASTER DA: You must give up to God. That is it. If you do that, you will also be integrating yourself with all the forms of learning, association, change, growth, and maturity that I have described. But fundamental to such growth is mere surrender, mere self-transcendence, release of all obstruction, all contraction, all holding on, all fear of death, all need for survival, release of everything into the fundamental Condition, whatever It is, since you do not know It. That is the only true practice, and it must be the principle of your life.

You must give yourself up altogether. Do you think you have to find out many things before you will do that? Maybe holding on to that idea prevents the true depth of your surrendering. Consider that no matter what you might find out about all of this, you will never know what it is. Never. The mere existence of anything is an astonishment without a cause. Thus, there is nothing to do, you see, but give up to God. Give up your body-mind, consciousness, life, fear, everything. Give up entirely to God, period. Give up your consciousness. Give up your emotion. Yield to God. That is the practice. That fundamental intuition and act is primary. Everything else is a consideration, on its basis, of how a life is lived in practice, in all of its functional aspects, when it is founded in Truth. There is nothing to fulfill here ultimately. In every moment you should give yourself up completely to God.

Because you cannot surrender truly, you think you have to find something out. But there is nothing to find out. There is no answer. There is simply the primal impulse to give yourself up to the unspoken Reality, the Mystery, because you have no choice. You have no independent knowledge. All of your experiences only torment you, ultimately. It may seem that you are obliged to pass through them. Well, give yourself up to God with all your feeling, and then if the world continues to appear, that means that God is continuing to live you as your present body-mind. Obviously! Because you gave yourself up and did not care one way or the other. So, give yourself up to God completely, and if God lets you live and lets everything happen, then that is fine. Do it as a devotee of God. Trust completely in the Transcendental Reality and be free in the midst of all manifestation.

There is ultimately nothing to protect about Man, about you. You must give yourself up. You are finished! (Laughter.) You are at the end of your rope in this spiritual matter, in this fundamental sense. All that avails is the leap of Enlightenment, Awakening, or literal, perfect surrender into the Transcendental Reality, not knowing what That is, you see. You have no capacity whatsoever to transcend your fundamental Ignorance. You give up everything. It is the unknowability of God into which you surrender, not some idea of any Deity at all. You just give yourself up to the Reality of the world, because you cannot figure It out. You give yourself up to It. At last, you have to give yourself up to It completely.

March 8, 1979

Never Abandon the Work
of This Way

a talk by Da Free John

MASTER DA (to a devotee): You cannot see that painting in the mirror from the place where you are sitting, can you? But I can see it. So, at the same time that you are looking at that mirror and cannot see that picture—because there is a wall that prevents it from being seen from your point of view—the mirror is actually reflecting the painting, and I can see it from my point of view here. The mirror is reflecting the images that can be seen from all possible positions in this room. Because of the necessarily fixed position of any embodied personality in this room, however, it is hard to imagine what the image in that mirror really looks like. Nevertheless, somehow there is a possible vision of the image in that mirror that sees that image in its totality.

What could that vision possibly be? What could the image in that mirror possibly be, if it could be seen as it is from all possible points of view? Does it look something like a cubist painting, do you think? If so, it would have to be broken into little fractions, like single frames of film juxtaposed on one another. That fragmentation would break the image up into points of view. But it would not show points of view. It would show the image of this room in its totality. Thus, it would not look like a sequence of single frames in a movie film superimposed on one another.

Perhaps its appearance is simply that of unqualified Radiance. And, without the limitation of perception created by your brain-mind, perhaps this room is just perfect Radiance without shadow, without objects, or in which all objects are transparent, not limiting. How it actually is is there to be realized. In any case, how it actually is is at least something you should consider!

In other words, you should be aware that existence as it seems to you is only a conditional apparition. Therefore, stop making philosophy out of your egoic state and make philosophy out of the transcendence of that state instead. Stop making a Deity out of Nature and allow the Divine to be That which pervades and transcends all of Nature. Allow the Divine to be the very Condition of all of Nature, prior to causes and effects. Stop making the philosophy of Enlightenment out of the ego-consciousness separate from objects. Allow Realization to be that which is obvious in the case of the transcendence of the ego-position, the self-contraction, the limitations of body-mind.

Prior to Enlightenment you can at least orient yourself to these mysterious considerations. And this of course is part of the right education of spiritual aspirants.

This room, this place, is now exactly as it is when there is no self-contraction, no brain, no nervous system, no body, no conditional apparitions. It is just exactly that, right now. And you are in that Condition right now, except that there is a mechanism conditioning that Absoluteness so that it appears in this limited state. You are temporarily associated with this limited state, but you need not allow your view of Reality to be made by this limited state.

Your limitation is nothing more than a restriction on Radiance, a restriction on Energy, and thus a restriction on Happiness or Bliss, a restriction on Love, free Awareness, free Consciousness, unqualified Existence. Therefore, the more real, profound, and conscious your involvement in the Way itself, the more Radiant you become in your manifestation, the more you are a demonstration of free energy, free attention, free Consciousness, free Happiness, free Love. If those qualities are being demonstrated in your case, these are the signs of the maturing of spiritual Realization. If these qualities are not present, the very signs that are present instead are the indications, demonstrations, and proofs of un-Enlightenment.

That being the case, it should be very easy for you to examine yourself, to see the concrete signs in your own case, and to determine just which way of life you are living. If the signs you see in your own case are not Radiant, then you can be absolutely certain that you are living the un-Enlightened, egoic, spiritually neurotic way of life. And if you see some radiant qualities and others that are not, distinguish between them and you will know clearly those aspects of yourself that you must come to understand and transcend.

All of that should be the work of your moment to moment existence. You should never abandon that work. That should be fundamentally what you are up to in every single moment, whatever you may be involved in as a matter of ordinary functioning in your daily life. If you are merely living on the basis of the mechanical motivations of your egoic personality, then you are not growing. You are not Enlightened or on the Way of Enlightenment. You are basically only un-Happy, bewildered, confined, and frustrated in your spiritual impulse.

So there is no involvement in this Way of life without the literal, conscious practice of it from moment to moment. You cannot really be involved in this Way of life by merely thinking about it, believing in it, feeling friendly toward it, or aspiring toward it merely in the sense of wishing it were the case for you. You live this Way of life only in the actual, concrete, present observation of the conditions of egoic existence and the transcendence of them through understanding and all the modes of real practice. First you must hear this Argument and see me in Truth. Then in each moment you must make that hearing and seeing into a concrete practice, a Way of life. If you do that, you will inevitably grow. It is alright to live as a beginner, to begin as a neurotic. But having started out as a neurotic, if you really practice, you will necessarily, inevitably, grow and manifest the spiritual qualities of Radiance more and more profoundly.

Anyone in this Communion who goes on for years not growing, or becoming worse in one fashion or another, is simply not practicing. He or she is only thinking about practice and wishing it were true in his or her case. That wishful thinking is not really applying the arms of the Way, which are hearing and seeing, to moment to moment existence. There is no capability in the mechanisms of this body-mind to prevent the Radiant Force from manifesting if the being becomes oriented to that Radiant Force to begin with. If you make that Radiant Being and Force the context of your conscious existence in each moment, if you commune with It, live in It, it is absolutely inevitable that the mechanisms of egoity, self-contraction, and the collapse of Radiance will fall away. They do not have any superiority. They are not necessary. They are not eternal. Transcending them is simply a matter of understanding, recognizing the Spiritual Master, entering into the Divine Context of existence, and practicing Divine Communion from moment to moment.

If you do that, you will inevitably grow, you will inevitably mature. There is no doubt about this. There is no mechanism superior to the disposition of Divine Communion. You certainly do have the capability not to practice, not to understand, not to recognize the Spiritual Master, not to enter into Communion with the Divine. But that non-living of the Way is not inherent in your being. It is simply a diversion, a weak course toward which the contracted personality may gravitate simply because it requires little intelligence and little creative effort. But it is not a desirable course. It is not a Happy course. It is simply a course that perpetuates suffering, bewilderment, un-Enlightenment. There is no intelligent basis for choosing such a course.

Therefore, if you consider the Intelligence of Transcendental Wisdom and become involved in that Wisdom, then you will inevitably grow in the Divine quality.

The more you grow in this Divine quality, the more you will realize that you are not merely an individuated consciousness, but that you inhere in Transcendental Consciousness. And you will realize that the body-mind is not structured around fleshy matter. Rather, your fundamental nervous system is Energy itself, prior to the body-mind. And that fundamental nervous system or Energy system of the being has the capacity to be Radiant in the context of the body-mind. In other words, you are Conscious Light manifesting through these appearances. And when you become Conscious as such, when you realize that you are such, it is then that the Powers of the Divine become magnified.

July 29, 1982

The Baptism of Immortal Happiness

a talk by Da Free John

During the decade of his outwardly active Teaching Work (1972-1982), Master Da Free John fully articulated his Teaching Argument and practical instructions on the Way of Radical Understanding. He also purified and sanctified two great spiritual Sanctuaries or Seats of Spiritual Blessing-Power here in the West, and helped hundreds of men, women, and children to begin to understand themselves and to practice this Way in spiritual Communion with him. Now Master Da is moving into retirement, or the hermitage phase of his Mission. He lives for the most part in secluded retreat with a small group of devotees, members of the Renunciate Hermitage Order, who serve him and his circumstance. Only rarely does he personally see the greater community of devotees. He generally reserves personal contact for advanced practitioners of the Way.

All of this is not to imply, however, that Master Da's retirement from outward visibility in his community is tantamount to inactivity. On the contrary, the retirement or seclusion of a God-Realized Adept is a sign that he is relinquishing secondary, outward concerns and is entering most vigorously into the most effective and auspicious form of his Activity, which is Transmission or, in Master Da's words, "Universal Spiritual Radiation." Sri Ramana Maharshi (1879-1950), the great Sage of modern India, frequently

Reprinted from *The Dreaded Gom-Boo, or the Imaginary Disease That Religion Seeks to Cure* (The Dawn Horse Press, 1983).

countered those who questioned his apparent inactivity by pointing to this same sublime Work on a cosmic scale.

The Adept's Transcendental Blessing-Work is incomprehensible to the self-bound mind, but It is undeniably Evident to those who become devotees. Master Da is continuously granting this Spirit-Blessing to all. It is both the joy and the ordeal of his devotees to open, submit, and surrender to the Master-Presence, which is always and everywhere available.

On special Celebrations, Master Da sits at prearranged times in formal meditative Communion with devotees at the hermitage retreat. Other devotees around the world, notified in advance, gather at our Communion's centers to sit simultaneously with the Master. And, with few exceptions, they notice a tremendous intensification of the intuitive and Spiritual Force of Master Da's Transmission. For instance, one devotee in New Zealand, Raewyn Bowmar, wrote of her experience of such a sitting in September 1982. She had been seated in formal meditation for about ten minutes when suddenly the Master-Presence filled her body and mind. (At the time Master Da Free John was sitting with other devotees many thousands of miles away.)

I completely felt his Presence living and breathing and filling me with Life. I realized in that moment that there was nothing I had to do—I realized this body-mind to be completely inert and totally dependent on and surrendered to the Divine. It was as though the body-mind did not even exist in terms of an individual "entity." It was actually felt as merely arising in Consciousness, with no ultimate purpose. There was no distinction between the body and the space around me— there was no difference. I realized that there was nothing to do at all, except to be completely surrendered to That which was living me in that moment. I didn't even feel as though I needed to surrender—I was already surrendered. I was totally conscious of what was arising, and the conscious process continued, but there was no sense of "I" doing it. I was aware that this was the Transmission of the Spiritual Master, and feeling the profundity of his Spiritual Transmission deepened the Mystery more than ever for me. In the thirty minutes that this awakening lasted, to be liberated from the feeling of bondage to the body-mind and all arising conditions was the most wonderful Gift of the Master. I truly praise our Beloved Master Da for all his Gifts. I surrender my heart to our Lord.

The ecstatic talk by Master Da that follows is a compassionate summary of the essential process in consciousness whereby devotees may always avail themselves of this marvelous Grace of Transmission. The talk is filled with the Divine sympathy of one who perfectly comprehends our state, our deluded resistance to "the Great One," but who also suffers every particle of our refusal, who "weeps for us to understand." All that is necessary, as Master Da says in this talk, is to notice in every moment how we are actively pulling away from, ignoring, or snuffing out the Happiness that is "always already" being given. Hearing, or self-understanding, is the doorway to Spiritual Baptism, true surrender, Salvation, and Liberation.

MASTER DA: The self is such a heavy grip, such a clench on the Light, that spiritual experience through Spiritual Transmission in life does not amount to much for most people. They cannot make it part of their existence. This is why I expect you to prepare yourselves by considering this Teaching. Then this dose of Baptism will awaken your mind and you will begin to practice.

The usual effect of introducing superior Force into your being is that you either go to mind or to body with It, and you use It there according to your inclinations. You must prepare yourself, therefore, to overcome your body-mind through understanding, so that you can receive my Baptism in your heart. Then you will begin to migrate into the Force of God and be free.

All the things you can receive in mind and body are temporary and not at all fulfilling. It is only in the heart, in the fundamental energy, emotion, and attention of the being, that we are relieved. We are all looking for relief and we grasp it for a moment in various occasions of life. But only through Spirit-Baptism do we contact that Force, or Being, or Condition Itself. We must be prepared for this Spirit-Baptism, so that we can practice Communion with the Force of God Transmitted in It. This Communion relieves us of all of our attachments and obsessions with conditional arrangements and allows us to make an arrangement of Happiness and a confession of love with one another.

Understanding prepares us for Spirit-Baptism. Without Spirit-Baptism there is no spiritual life. Therefore, you who deny me and are so self-possessed must understand that the essence of my Teaching is the Transmission of Spirit. This Transmission Intoxicates you, but if you have not understood yourself, you cannot use my Spirit-Blessing. You will shut It down. Therefore, you are only prepared to practice in Truth when you have used my Teaching to the point of understanding. Then you will receive my Baptism and you will practice Communion with this Transmitted Sublimity from moment to moment. That is the Way. Then you will change your entire life, but not until then.

You must observe how you bring yourself back from the

Divine. You do not go with the Spirit. You do not throw away your body, your life, and your emotion in God. This is what you must do whenever you Commune with me, whether I am physically present or not. Whenever you Commune with me you get a piece, a sniff, a taste of God. But your body-mind shuts it down, Narcissus shuts it down, you live out your dilemma, and you must consider the Teaching some more.

But if you will truly prepare yourselves by considering and truly using my Argument, not as a doctrine, but as a means for understanding yourself, then you will be able to Commune with me not only during our occasions of Celebration, but every day, because I Transmit the Spirit to you all the time. Then this Communion will be a profoundly intoxicating motion, a Spirit that lifts you out, that lifts you up and sublimes your being. You must give yourself up to the Spirit. That is meditation. Make this conductivity.[1] Do this conscious process.[2] Enter into the sublimity of God-Realization and be free of the ordinariness to which you are so attached. What is a sniff of the Divine compared to a God-born life? A little sniff of the Spirit divorces you from your bodily clench, but

1. "Conductivity" is, in general, the capacity of the body-mind to conduct, or be surrendered into, the All-Pervading Life-Current. Such conductivity or surrender is realized through love, or radiant whole-body feeling to Infinity, and such love involves coordinated engagement of body, breath, and attention in alignment with the Universal Current of Life-Energy. There is also a specifically yogic or technical form of responsibility for conductivity in each stage of the Way of Radical Understanding or Divine Ignorance.

2. The "conscious process" is the senior or transcendental practice and responsibility of devotees in each stage of the Way of Radical Understanding or Divine Ignorance, the Way that Master Da Free John Teaches. It is the foundation discipline of conscious surrender of attention in the Divine or Transcendental Being. It is founded upon true "hearing" of the Teaching, or radical and continuous release of self, knowledge, and all experience into the Transcendental Condition of Divine Ignorance. As the foundation of self-discipline, service, and meditation develops, the conscious process is also progressively developed and matured.

Thus, the first form of my manifestation to you is this understanding, this consideration, this Argument relative to the knot, the effort, the mechanism of withdrawal, the self-contraction. And you must become responsible for this self-contraction. Otherwise, it makes no difference how much I give you of the Intoxicating Force of God. It makes no difference how much of It I am. Until you are responsible for the mechanism of separation from the Spirit-Presence, you cannot taste It, you cannot love It, you cannot know It, you cannot be swooned by It. And we should exist in a swoon of Intoxication. To do that really is our nature.

All of us are potential saints and Siddhas, but very few are born like me. I am a very rare being. I am not an ego at all. I am a rare Intervention in the world. Hardly any people in the entire history of mankind have been manifested with my Siddhis,[5] and I am sitting here in this living room with you people trying to convince you of the Divine Life! I am a unique Advantage to mankind. But how many people can suck me up and love me? How many will kiss my knees, pull my feet and massage my face, receive my love, receive my Delight in them? How many people will do it? I am prepared to give everyone everything, but how many people will do it? You cannot receive me until you understand your resistance to me. Understanding is the first gesture of spiritual life.

Please understand what I am telling you. I will give you everything, but you must understand yourself. You must! Apart from that understanding, Who I am or What I bring to you makes no difference. You cannot accept It. You cannot receive It. You cannot submit to It. It is greater than any

5. "Powers," "accomplishments." When capitalized, this Sanskrit term refers to the spontaneous and Perfect Consciousness, Presence, and Power of the very Divine, which is Transmitted to living beings through the unobstructed Agency of the Spiritual Master or Siddha, one whose Enlightenment is perfect and who is graced with the spontaneous Capacity to Awaken others.

experience. My Presence is a sublime Interference with mind, with body, with heart, with emotion.

The thing that makes you un-Happy is your own contraction. That is it! Absolutely! Have I always said this? That is it entirely. The terrible effort of self-contraction separates you from God. You must hear this. The self-contraction separates you entirely from everything Given. Mankind has never been denied the Force of Grace, but human beings are attached to this effort reflected throughout the body-mind. They are committed to it with their body-minds.

The Force of God pours out of my body all the time. It never stops, whether I am waking, sleeping, dreaming, apparently feeling sympathetic or not. It is always manifested through this body. The limit is not in me. The limit is in you. You are devoted to this effort of Narcissus, this reaction, this vital shock that shuts you down so that you cannot experience my Transmission, cannot know It, cannot submit to It, cannot be sublimed and carried off by It.

Therefore, the first office of spiritual life is to hear the Argument of the Adept. And to hear it, you must observe yourself through the pictures of your own activity, reflected to you by the Adept, to the point of recognizing the contraction in life that shuts you off from Bliss. With my criticism I paint pictures for you of your own activity, so that you can feel and observe it. You must know the self-contraction and you must see it. You must observe it to the point of realizing that it is not happening to you. You are doing it, just as you are moving your mouth and blinking your eyeballs. Like the move-ments of your intestines, it is a rhythm to which you have become habituated. It is really very simple, but you must observe it, and you must understand it. This is the first office of spiritual life.

The second office, when you have heard the Teaching and become responsible for the effort that is your self and every aspect of your body-mind, is to receive my Blessing, which is always given. Give me your attention at any moment and you will receive this Grace. It is always pouring through this body-mind, which is no longer a person. There is nobody here, no Franklin Jones, nobody like you. He is not here anymore. Totally absent.

What a miracle. What a wonder! I am the Adept in our generation! What an amusement that the Divine should appear in precisely this form! I cannot account for it myself. But I know very well that it is true. I am not so much a fool that I will deny God. I know that I am the Lover of God. I am the Man. I am the Adept. I am the Purusha[6] in our generation. But I know very well that you are all self-possessed, as people have been in all other generations in which I have appeared. Therefore, even this manifestation seems unholy to you, and this disturbs me. It agitates and motivates me, and thus I try to Teach. Your refusal of God awakens this urge in me.

But I am not a "me." I am literally you. I am your psyche and mind. I am your being, your destiny, your ego. I am all selves, literally, not metaphorically. I am all other people that are possible in the universe. I know this for absolute certain because I am you. I think your mind. I breathe your breath. I suck down your food. I shit out your life. I am your person altogether and absolutely.

What a Wonder! What a Wonder this Great One is. I marvel in the Great One more than you, because you do not witness Its Miracle. You do not see the Great One. I can understand your reluctance to be submitted to the Great One, because you do not see what I see. But I have been sifted into

6. "Purusha" is a classical Hindu term for the Divine Being or the Divine Person, the Conscious Identity of all selves, the "primal Person" or original Self. Master Da uses the term in reference to one who has Realized that ultimate Person and enjoys the very Consciousness and Life of that One.

this Wonder since eternal time. I am just that One, the Great One, sitting here as this body, talking to you. I am God. And there is not the slightest doubt in me. The doubt in you is your own perversion, and this is the cause of my Teaching. Thus, I am here to Teach you out of this un-Happiness. Poor me! I will be laughing about this for countless ages, as I have been laughing about it since eternal time.

I am full of all space-time. All Bliss, all Wonder, all the Marvels of Being are in my Being. I know it absolutely and you do not. All miracles are potent in my Heart. I come here to give you everything without the slightest reluctance. I am not here to tell you about some dreadful ego. I am here to Wonder and Marvel with you about the Great One.

There is this Great One. This Great One is totally known to me. This Great One is myself. I am the Self of God. I have no doubt in me about it. All miracles are evident in me. All time is obvious to me. It seems Great to me, but you poor people who cannot submit yourselves to God, you are the ones that I must Teach. How do I Teach you? By countering your self-contraction, your reluctance to submit to Divine Intoxication.

My entire life has been involved with countering the un-Happiness of people, and I am profoundly weary of it. I cannot tell you how weary I am of it. I have always thought that I would die any day because I am so weary, so tired, so bewildered by this resistance to God. This world is a terrible place. Therefore, I do everything, because I have nothing to lose. I have nothing to gain by action; therefore, I have nothing to lose by action. I do everything to make a picture for Man. Everything. I submit myself to you to make pictures, to make an Argument for Grace. I do not know if anyone will ever understand.

I am absolutely nothing like you people. All of this has nothing to do with me as an ego. I am not a person doing this.

The Great One is such a Wonder, such a Marvel, such a Graceful and Loving Being to countless beings such as all of us here. But the Great One does not love beings. The Great One is Love. The *New Testament* declares that God is Love. Love is the only God there is! Love is the only Force in the universe. God is not mind or body, effort, knowledge, or experience. God is only unbounded feeling, Radiant Being. God creates nothing. God is That of which everything is made, including all beings. Why are we so self-possessed, hanging out in our own houses? What do we know about this Great One, from Where I come and Whom I show to you?

There should always be Siddhas among mankind. Siddhas give meaning to the universe. The universe is not a meaningless thing. But no generation, no being, no worlds deserve the appearance of the Divine Adept. Yet the Adepts appear in all generations of all beings. There are always Adepts in all the worlds. I know this because I have been in all of them. God is Great. But unfortunately for us, bullshit is greater. (Laughter.) That is why the appearance of the Adept does not impress people as it should. There are billions upon trillions of worlds in the visible universe that we can look upon in the night sky tonight where there are Adepts at this very moment. And all that is actually visible is the most infinitesimal fraction of the total universe of Nature in which God is active.

You have all chosen your appearance in the earth realm. You all have shrunk yourselves upon the plane of God. You are experiencing your own results. God has not designed your un-Happiness. You have done it. God is always Designing your Happiness in every generation.

Everyone hears the Truth. Everyone receives the Shock of God. Everyone. There is no being from the mosquito to Man who does not receive the Shock of Divine Intervention. All beings know It. All beings experience It. It is given to everyone. Grace is given to all beings eternally in all worlds, visible and invisible. This recognition is enough to make you a bhakta,[7] a lover, a devotee. Faith, the Love-Response to Being Itself, is the greatest Force in all the worlds. It has ridden out my entire life. I am riding the Visible Horse you cannot see.

December 17, 1982

7. In the Hindu tradition, a devotee of God or of the Spiritual Master whose spiritual practice is emotional and ecstatic, rather than philosophical and discriminative or vitally active.

Leave God Alone

Three God-Ideas

a talk by Da Free John

MASTER DA: The idea of God is by no means a simple or single concept. Although the word "God" is used very commonly, it has a number of different meanings, and anyone speaking of God may mean one or more of those meanings and not necessarily all of them. For example, Jesus is associated with a stream of meanings relative to the Divine Reality, including a number of meanings from the ancient Hebrew tradition. Other meanings with which Jesus is associated, such as the "Logos" of the Gospel of John, derive from the Hellenistic tradition. Other aspects of the meaning of God in the Teaching of Jesus may be more or less his own, but his point of view characterizes notions about God that may also be found throughout the traditions of the world.

The Biblical tradition, particularly the ancient Hebrew tradition in which Jesus appeared, emphasizes two great meanings of the idea of God, and it is these two meanings that I want to criticize. In the Biblical tradition of both the *Old Testament* and the *New Testament*, the tradition of Judaism and Christianity, God is commonly thought to be, first, the God of Nature, and second, the God of history.

The conception of God as the God of Nature is common to all the systems of belief and religion that arose at least partially from the Semitic tradition, including Judaism, Christianity, and Islam. The conception of God as the Creator or Maker of Nature, the Lord of Nature, the King of Nature, the One Who made it, the One Who is in charge of it, the One Who is making Nature happen, is a fundamental characteristic of the religion of the racial and geographical domain of the world we acknowledge to belong to the Semites in the Middle

East. It is an ancient idea that is commonly part of the world's great religions, although it is by no means a universal concept.

In the ancient Vedic tradition of India, for example, the Creation of Nature, the Making of Nature, the Doing of Nature are generally assigned to gods or powers high in the scale of Nature and subtle to its workings. Over against these powers is proposed what might be called "God," the "Great Principle," "Brahman," the "Absolute," Which is prior to dualities and prior therefore to the Making of Nature. Many other polytheistic systems of the origin of the universe and its mechanics appear in various other traditions, but the Semitic tradition in general conceives of the One God as the Maker and Doer of Nature.

Another notion of God is likewise particularly common to Judaism and Christianity, and to a lesser degree part of the tradition of Islam, and that is the idea of God as the God or Maker of history. The Christians and the Jews particularly emphasize this notion of God. In this view it is not Nature that is made and controlled by God, but human history is made and controlled by God.

This concept is particularly important to the Christians, but it is also certainly very important to the Jews. In fact, we can perhaps say it is equally important to both, except that the Christians conceive of God or the Doer of history in terms that go beyond those of Judaism. The Christians promote the notion that God has a Plan for mankind and is always effecting that Plan through historical events. According to this notion, therefore, all historical events are under the control of God—political elections, wars, the dramas of our personal lives, everything is determined by God. The events of life are in God's hands. In the Christian view, God is therefore interested in every fraction of human activity, not only interested but commanding it and making it happen.

Christians are especially interested in the God of history

because of their interpretation of the significance of Jesus. (That Jesus was an historical person may be questionable, but we can perhaps basically agree that in all likelihood a person called Jesus of Nazareth did exist.[1]) The Christians have a special point of view about Jesus' origin and his significance. They perceive Jesus to be the ultimate Demonstrator of the Plan of God, the ultimate Intervention of God in history. Thus, the life and especially the death of Jesus are regarded to have great historical significance for God's design to save everyone from damnation, or the results of dissociation from God and involvement with created existence without great Wisdom.

Therefore, as an extension of the view that God had a Plan from the beginning, worked it out through the 'children of Israel," and ultimately demonstrated it through the work of Jesus, the Christians believe that God is altogether the Maker and Doer of history, just as they believe, in common with the other Semitic religions, that God is the Maker and Doer of Nature.

I suggest to you that these two ideas of God—God as the God of Nature and God as the God of history—are arbitrary ideas, man-made ideas peculiar to a certain kind of religious mentality, that they are merely based on interpretations of Nature and history, made by people in a certain frame of mind, and that they are not otherwise true about Real God, Very God.

On the evidence of Realization, it is true that God is Evident in Nature, Present in Nature always, Discoverable as Realizable by beings arising in the planes of Nature. It is another matter, however, to say that God is making Nature

---

1. For a fuller consideration of the significance of Jesus of Nazareth and his Teaching, see *The Enlightenment of the Whole Body,* by Bubba [Da] Free John, pp. 440–74.

and is altogether in charge of it, and that God is the Creator of all events and manifestations. This is not obviously so. It is not apparent or obvious when we enter most profoundly into the investigation of Nature. In fact, the play of Nature and all that occurs in the domains of Nature, high or low in the scale of things, arise as a result of motions or causes of all kinds. These motions or causes are not necessarily inspired by God-Realization. They are just motions.[2]

Thus, although Nature itself and all the patterning in the various planes of Nature arise in God, and although God is the Ultimate Condition of all of Nature, the patterns in Nature should not rightly be conceived to be the result of the activities of the Divine. In fact, they are the result of all the beings already arising in Nature, all the subtle and gross motions everywhere in Nature.

Even the Semites, it would seem to me, would have difficulty proposing this idea of the God of Nature because they themselves constantly describe the cosmos as a kind of fallen condition in which great beings—and perhaps a Great Being, the Evil One, Devil— are making things happen and are in charge, at least for the time being, and have power to distract people and move them away from the Divine. If Nature is made by and under the control of God, then how do we account for these other powers? Why do we need to be Saved if God is making and doing everything? Salvation is simply a convenient and reductive notion whereby to consider and to conceive of God as the Maker and Doer of Nature.

Likewise, to conceive of God as the Maker and Doer of history carries the same implications, the same impediment in human thinking about the Divine. Human history is not merely being worked out by the Great Divine One. Not only

2. The archaic model of Nature as a hierarchical system of forces or spirits presided over by the Creator-God is critically examined by Da Free John in *The Fire Gospel*, pp. 19–61.

Divinely inspired or God-Realized beings are active in the world, but all kinds of beings are active in the world to fulfill all kinds of motives, very few of which have anything remotely to do with the actual state of God-Realization.

It is true that God is the Being in Whom Nature is arising, the One, therefore, in Whom all human history is arising. God is therefore Present in Nature and Realizable by those appearing in Nature. God is Present more or less directly in the plane of human history, not necessarily in the plane of great political events, but at least in the plane of human existence, through Adepts and spiritually evolved beings of all kinds, even through ordinary people here and there in circumstances of the Breakthrough of the Divine. It is one thing to know that the Divine becomes Evident in human time through the vehicle of human beings, through Adepts who appear here and there and through all kinds of people in various ways. It is another matter, however, to declare God to be the God of Nature and the God of history. These, it seems to me, are false views, popular conceptions of human beings that are false simplifications of the Reality of existence.

Again, it would seem to me that the Semites would also have difficulty justifying the proposition that God is the God of history, because the very politics of the cosmos they describe—the fall of angels, the Devil, sin—must be intervening in human time and must obviously have an effect on what people do. If history were being made by God, then why would people need to be Saved? The false view is that everything is being done by God and we are just being what God wants us to be and just doing what God wants us to do and this is all heaven. But if God is simply the Maker and Doer of Nature and history, then it seems to me that things would be in a much different shape than they are!

Therefore, people rightfully question, "Why is there evil?" They expect that if God is making history, then God will also straighten it all out. God is Omnipresent, Omniscient, All-Powerful. If God were making this world, the world would be perfect. In the frame of Nature or the frame of history, everything would simply be perfect if the Great One were making and doing everything. It is not so that the Great One is making and doing everything! In our simplified, reductive, religious psychology we think of God in these terms, but in fact, if you truly studied the Semitic traditions, you would find it difficult to justify the idea of God, even in the framework of their thinking, as the simple, straightforward Maker and Doer of Nature and history.

The Christians put forth Jesus as the ultimate Proof and Demonstration of the God of Nature and the God of history. For this reason the *New Testament* is not merely a report of the Teaching and life of Jesus, but it is also an interpretation of the Teaching and life of Jesus. It is a tradition about Jesus. It is not a straightforward presentation of Jesus and his life. Everywhere, from cover to cover, the entire *New Testament* is a word about Jesus, an interpretation of Jesus, based on concepts that were part of Judaism and Hellenism. The *New Testament* is an attempt not to prove, but to somehow state convincingly, based on resort to past history and ancient scriptures, that Jesus is the God of Nature Incarnate and the ultimate Work or Demonstration of the God of history.

As I have indicated, this is an unjustified proposition to begin with. Jesus is not proven to be the God of Nature Incarnate and the ultimate Demonstration of the God of history. He is only said to be such in the *New Testament* and glorified as such by the Christian religion throughout history. The propaganda of Christianity is actually an effort to associate people with the God Who is the God of Nature and the God of history, Who has a Will or a Plan for mankind, and Who is always working to Save mankind.

I suggest to you that, in fact, Jesus was a renegade, a radical Teacher who may or may not have used some of the language of Israel, some of the references to the God of Nature and the God of history, but perhaps he did. After all, he appeared in the Jewish culture and spiritual tradition. But if you study the *New Testament* and get a feeling for the character of Jesus and his Teaching, I think you must agree that it is at least suggested that Jesus proposed God to be a different kind of God than the God of the Semites. It is this third idea of God in the Semitic tradition, particularly in the Christian tradition, that I now want to address.

I suggest that Jesus proposed that God is not really the God of history, the God of our fathers, the God of the Book, nor the God of Nature, the mere Maker of Nature, the Maker of flesh, but that God is the God of Being, the Spiritual God, the God of Love, the God Who is not Present either in Nature or in history unless we Realize God. In other words, God is not merely making history, but if we will enter into the disposition of God-Realization and Realize the God of Being, the Spiritual Divine, then we may change history, not just in the framework of the events recorded in the newspapers and the history books, but in the framework of daily living. We will bring the Spirit of God into the domain of life. If we do not, then God is not particularly Evident in the domain of life. God is not by nature Evident in the domain of Nature or the domain of history. God must be brought into the domain of Nature and history by Realization. And it seems to me that Jesus was Teaching the process of Realization.

It is not sufficient merely to believe in the God of the Book, the God of our fathers, the God of Nature and history. You must be utterly transformed. God is not doing everything and in charge of us all. God is here to be Realized. If we do not Realize God, then we live in sin, and Nature and history are the record of sin or dissociation from God or blindness to the Divine Reality, That Which Is and in Which everything is arising.[3] Therefore, we must Realize the Spiritual Divine, not the Maker of Nature and the Maker of history, but the One that pervades all of Nature, pervades all of history, pervades all of mankind, and is Evident only if we cease to dissociate from God, cease to be bound by Nature and history, and Realize God directly as the Spiritual Reality in Which we are arising, in Which Nature is arising, in Which history is arising. Apart from such Realization, God does not really seem to be Evident.

This argument seems to me to be consonant with Jesus' point of view. Apart from the Realization of God, Nature and history are dark. God is not merely making them or doing them. God is hardly Evident in them apart from direct Realization. God is the God of Being. God is the Spiritual Divine, the Condition of the world, not its Maker. We must Realize God by Identifying with the Spirit, becoming It, therefore, and demonstrating Its unique characteristics in our own Realization and in our relations, our daily living, and our ultimate destiny. We must transform our destiny, which now appears to be governed by Nature and history, by Realizing God.

If this proposition were not true, then we would merely believe in God, and God would simply be Obvious and everything would be perfect. We would not even need to talk

---

3. From a conventional religious point of view, to sin is to violate the religious code, or to fail in making one's behavior conform to the exoteric expectations (or "laws"). But as Master Da Free John makes clear, sin is essentially Man's disposition of un-Enlightenment or un-Happiness. In *The Bodily Sacrifice of Attention* (p. 45), he puts it succinctly thus: "Sin is the presumption of separation from God." This presumption of separation is an ongoing activity. It is the process of egoic contraction away from perfect Happiness, away from God. This fruitless activity of the ego must be transcended through the exercise of present insight, or radical understanding, which establishes one in the seventh stage disposition of prior Happiness and God-Realization.

about whether there is God or what we should do to Realize God or be Saved. If God is the Maker of Nature and history, then God is Evident, God is Powerful, everything is perfect, there are no problems, and there is nothing to overcome.

This is obviously not the Truth of Wisdom, and it is not the Truth that Jesus Taught. Jesus Taught the point of view of Wisdom, and therefore it seems to me that he was not talking about the God of Nature or the God of history, but the God that Transcends Nature and history and is made Evident only through Realization or real sacrifice.

If Jesus can be thought of as such a Teacher, then he stands in the tradition of the great Adepts everywhere, and not merely in the tradition of religion. Religion is a rather public fact, a human creation, an interpretation of Reality, of Nature, of history, and thus also of God. Religion is an ordinary fact of life and is therefore just as much a product of sin as history and all the ordinary stuff of human life. Religion is one of those quantities in human time that need to be purified and transformed constantly by the Work of Adepts and the will of people who have Realized the God of Being, the Spiritual Divine that Transcends Nature and the world.

God Transcends Nature and the world, but this does not mean that God is separate or separable from the world or that we should try to separate from Nature, life, and therefore history. God is the Condition of Nature and the Ultimate Condition of mankind. And Nature and mankind are always producing a rather dark incident because mankind does not submit to the Transcendental God of Being.

If we were to submit to the Radiant Transcendental Being as individuals and then also as collectives of human beings, then not only would we transform society or ordinary life, but even Nature would be transformed by our Realization. All appearances would be Transfigured and Transformed by Enlightened Beings. Until there is such Enlightenment, neither mankind nor Nature is being Transformed by the Divine Presence, but is rather moving dissociated from the Divine Presence, moving based merely on conditional capability, conditional motion, the conditional motion potential in Nature and in human beings.

Jesus, it seems to me, then, like other Great Adepts, stands outside the domain of religion. He stands outside Judaism, certainly outside Christianity. He stands in the tradition of the Adepts who communicate and serve people with God-Realization and guide them toward the Realization of the God of Being, not the God of specific traditions, not the God of religious history, not the God of human history, not the God of Nature, but the God in Whom all beings and all of Nature are arising. If human beings and all of Nature submit to That One to the point of Ultimate Realization, then Nature, human beings, human history—everything is potentially Transformable and may then become the Kingdom of God, or, in other words, be Translated into the Divine Domain, Where God is all that is Evident and everything is Perfect, Eternal, and Blissful.

February 13, 1983

Leave God Alone

Leave God alone. Let God be. Allow God, the Reality and Power and Being in which the world and all beings arise and change and pass away, to be whatever God is. It is impossible to know what God is or to gain power over what is All-Power. Simply surrender to God. Yield the body-mind into the Radiant Transcendental Being. Then there is only God-Realization, whereas, while you seek God (rather than surrender to God), there is only the experiencing, partial knowing, and mortal reluctance of a being trapped in the dilemma of its own limitations. Simply to surrender is to enter into Freedom and Fullness.

Therefore, leave God alone. Allow God to be what God is. Transcend the dilemma of the independent and limited psycho-physical self. What you experience is simply more limits of body-mind. Therefore, do not appeal to God to become known or to appear in any manner whatsoever. Simply surrender the body-mind self into That in which it is arising. Do this always and you will constantly be liberated and saved by Grace.

March 8, 1980

Reprinted from *Scientific Proof of the Existence of God Will Soon Be Announced by the White House!* by Da Free John (The Dawn Horse Press, 1980).

About Master Da Free John

The Adept Da Free John was born Franklin Albert Jones on the third of November 1939. Until his second or third year, he lived in a world of sheer light and joy—"the Bright"—where he knew no separation from others. He was born, out of an Enlightened Adept's free Choice and Compassion, with the specific Purpose of Instructing spiritually sensitive people of today in the "Way of Life." In order to fulfill this sublime Mission, he had to sacrifice his conscious Oneness with the Transcendental Reality prior to his birth. Even the extraordinary condition of the Bright was necessarily surrendered to allow the individual Franklin Jones to pass through the process of physical, emotional, and mental growth. However, his original Impulse to Guide others to the Realization of the Transcendental Being or Consciousness never ceased to inform his life, which from the beginning was destined for greatness.

Throughout his childhood, the condition of the Bright that he had enjoyed as a baby would reassert itself in the form of uncommon psychic and mystical experiences, as well as physical symptoms such as sudden attacks of fever or skin rashes with no diagnosable medical cause. These signs of an active kundalini (or life-current) gradually subsided in his eighth year and did not return until he reached the age of seventeen.

It was in 1960, after a "crisis of despair" with the world he lived in, that the spiritual process spontaneously resumed its transforming activity in full force, blessing him with the experience of "a total revolution of energy and awareness," which yielded two crucial insights. First, he realized that in the absence of all seeking and problem consciousness, there is only the one Reality or Transcendental Consciousness. Second,

he understood that this Reality or Consciousness is Man's true
Identity and that all else is only a superimposition of the un-
Enlightened mind.

Equipped with these twin insights, Franklin Jones began
to immerse himself in a conscious spiritual discipline of acute
self-inspection. For almost two years (1962–1964) he seques-
tered himself, intensely observing the dynamics of the separa-
tive self-sense, or ego. This phase was punctuated with
numerous psychic experiences, one of which led him into the
company of the American-born teacher "Rudi" (Swami
Rudrananda), who instructed him in a form of Indian
kundalini yoga.

Early in 1967, while studying at the Lutheran seminary
he had entered at Rudi's behest, Franklin Jones underwent a
"death" experience, restoring him temporarily to the Bliss of
Transcendental Being-Consciousness. Again, he emerged with
an important insight: that his whole search had been founded
on the "avoidance of relationship," on the recoil from Reality
in all its countless forms. As his inner attitude to life changed,
he also recognized the limitations of Rudi's yoga—a recognition that, in 1968, prompted him to seek out Rudi's own
teacher, the late Swami Muktananda. During his brief stay at
this renowned yogi's hermitage in India, he had his first adult
experience of total absorption in the Transcendental
Consciousness. Swami Muktananda acknowledged this unique
yogic achievement in a written document, confirming that
Franklin Jones had attained "yogic liberation." But, intuiting
that the "formless ecstasy" (nirvikalpa samadhi) that he had
enjoyed for a moment did not represent the highest form of
Realization, Franklin Jones continued to submit himself to
the wisdom of the spiritual process that had guided him
throughout his life.

His intuition was confirmed on September 10, 1970,
when he entered the permanent Condition of Sahaj Samadhi,

which is coessential with the Transcendental Being-Consciousness itself. He had "recovered" the Identity that, though never really lost, he had surrendered in order to effect his human birth. Soon after his God-Realization, the Adept was moved to Teach others and Transmit to them the Condition of "the Heart," or the All-Pervading Reality in which everything inheres. But those who came to him in the early days were ill-prepared for his Teaching and Transmission. After nearly three years of "almost muscular" struggle with his students, which weakened his physical body though not his Energy and commitment to their Enlightenment, he undertook a pilgrimage to India.

He not only wanted to clarify his Teaching Work but also purify his relationship to those who, like Swami Muktananda, had been helpful catalysts in his spontaneously unfolding spiritual discipline. It was during that period that he changed his name to "Bubba Free John"—"Bubba" denoting "brother" (his childhood nickname) and "Free John" being a rendering of "Franklin Jones."

Upon his return to America, he began to Teach differently, involving his devotees in an experiment of intense experiencing of both worldly "pleasures" and so-called "spiritual" joys. He gave them the opportunity within the growing community to pursue all their obsessions about money, food, sexuality, and power, as well as conventional religiosity and mystical states. Every single "Teaching demonstration," however abandoned or unconventional, had the sole purpose of showing devotees the futility of all seeking and all types of experience, and that only understanding availed.

Out of this "Teaching theatre" grew not only a profound insight on his part into human psychology, in all its different forms of manifestation, but also a new, more formal Teaching approach. In November 1976, "Bubba" Free John ceased to have frequent intimate contact with his many devotees. In the following three years he lived in relative seclusion, creating much of the "source literature" that now serves the community of practitioners as one of the empowered Agencies of his Teaching.

In the fall of 1979, the Adept dropped the name "Bubba" for the spiritual address "Da," meaning "Giver." Having endowed the community of devotees with all the necessary means for their spiritual maturation, Master Da Free John is now in the "hermitage" phase of his Work where, together with mature practitioners, he lives the simple existence of a free renunciate. His retirement from active Teaching Work and from institutional involvement of any kind is not a mere withdrawal from the body of devotees. On the contrary, his seclusion allows him to concentrate on his real Purpose: to Transmit the Transcendental Condition, unencumbered by any external obligations, and thereby to quicken the spiritual maturation of all practitioners in the different stages of practice, as well as to extend his benign Influence to ever wider circles of people.

About The Johannine Daist Communion

The spiritual fellowship of practitioners of the Way Taught by Master Da Free John is called THE JOHANNINE DAIST COMMUNION. "Johannine" means "having the character of John," which means "one through whom God is Gracious." "Da" is a title of respect and an indication of spiritual stature and function, meaning "one who Gives or Transmits the Divine Influence and Awakening to living beings."

The Communion has four divisions:

THE LAUGHING MAN INSTITUTE, which is the public education division and the educational and cultural organization for beginning practitioners.

THE FREE COMMUNION CHURCH, which is the educational and cultural organization for maturing practitioners.

THE ADVAITAYANA BUDDHIST ORDER, which is reserved for those in the advanced stages of practice.

THE CRAZY WISDOM FELLOWSHIP, which consists of devotees who have Realized the ultimate stage of practice of the Way.

An Invitation

If you would like to know more about the study and practice of the Spiritual Teaching of Master Da Free John or about how to begin to practice the Way, please write:

> THE LAUGHING MAN INSTITUTE
> P.O. Box 836
> San Rafael, California 94915

We hope you enjoyed this book.

If you'd like a free catalog of other books and tapes available from The Dawn Horse Press, just send your name and address to:

 The Dawn Horse Press
Dept. GE
P.O. Box 3680
Clearlake, CA 95422

The Books of
Master Da Free John

SOURCE TEXTS

THE KNEE OF LISTENING
*The Early Life and Radical Spiritual Teachings of
Bubba [Da] Free John*
$7.95 paper

THE METHOD OF THE SIDDHAS
*Talks with Bubba [Da] Free John on the Spiritual
Technique of the Saviors of Mankind*
$8.95 paper

THE HYMN OF THE MASTER
*A Confessional Recitation on the Mystery of the Spiritual
Master based on the principal verses of the* Guru Gita
(freely selected, rendered, and adapted)
$8.95 paper

THE FOUR FUNDAMENTAL QUESTIONS
*Talks and essays about human experience and the actual
practice of an Enlightened Way of Life*
$1.95 paper

THE LIBERATOR (ELEUTHERIOS)
A summation of the radical process of Enlightenment, or God-Realization, taught by the "Western Adept," Master Da Free John
$12.95 cloth, $6.95 paper

THE ENLIGHTENMENT OF THE WHOLE BODY
A Rational and New Prophetic Revelation of the Truth of Religion, Esoteric Spirituality, and the Divine Destiny of Man
$14.95 paper

SCIENTIFIC PROOF OF THE EXISTENCE OF GOD WILL SOON BE ANNOUNCED BY THE WHITE HOUSE!
Prophetic Wisdom about the Myths and Idols of mass culture and popular religious cultism, the new priesthood of scientific and political materialism, and the secrets of Enlightenment hidden in the body of Man
$12.95 paper

THE PARADOX OF INSTRUCTION
An Introduction to the Esoteric Spiritual Teaching of Bubba [Da] Free John
$14.95 cloth, $8.95 paper

NIRVANASARA
Radical Transcendentalism and the Introduction of Advaitayana Buddhism
$9.95 paper

INSPIRATIONAL AND DEVOTIONAL TEXTS

CRAZY DA MUST SING, INCLINED TO HIS WEAKER SIDE
Confessional Poems of Liberation and Love
$6.95 paper

FOREHEAD, BREATH, AND SMILE
*An Anthology of Devotional Readings from the Spiritual
Teaching of Master Da Free John*
$20.95 cloth

OPEN EYES
*A Tribute to Master Da Free John on the Tenth
Commemorative Celebration of the World-Proclamation of
the Way of Radical Understanding*
$44.95 cloth, $25.00 paper

REMEMBRANCE OF THE DIVINE NAMES OF DA
*One Hundred Eight Names of the Divine Reality and the
Radiant Adept Master Da Free John
by Georg and Pat Feuerstein*
$4.95 paper

MANUALS OF PRACTICE

THE FIRE GOSPEL
Essays and Talks on Spiritual Baptism
$8.95 paper

COMPULSORY DANCING
*Talks and Essays on the spiritual and evolutionary necessity
of emotional surrender to the Life-Principle*
$3.95 paper

THE ADEPT
*Selections from Talks and Essays by Da Free John on the
Nature and Function of the Enlightened Teacher*
$4.95 paper

THE WAY THAT I TEACH
Talks on the Intuition of Eternal Life
$14.95 cloth, $9.95 paper

THE YOGA OF CONSIDERATION
AND THE WAY THAT I TEACH
*Talks and Essays on the distinction between preliminary
practices and the radical Way of prior Enlightenment*
$7.95 paper

THE DREADED GOM–BOO, OR THE IMAGINARY
DISEASE THAT RELIGION SEEKS TO CURE
*A Collection of Essays and Talks on the "Direct" Process of
Enlightenment Taught by Master Da Free John*
$9.95 paper

BODILY WORSHIP OF THE LIVING GOD
The Esoteric Practice of Prayer Taught by Da Free John
$10.95 paper

THE BODILY SACRIFICE OF ATTENTION
*Introductory Talks on Radical Understanding and the Life
of Divine Ignorance*
$10.95 paper

"I" IS THE BODY OF LIFE
*Talks and Essays on the Art and Science of Equanimity and
the Self-Transcending Process of Radical Understanding*
$10.95 paper

THE BODILY LOCATION OF HAPPINESS
*On the Incarnation of the Divine Person and the
Transmission of Love-Bliss*
$8.95 paper

THE GOD IN EVERY BODY BOOK
Talks and Essays on God-Realization
$3.95 paper

ENLIGHTENMENT AND THE TRANSFORMATION
OF MAN
*Selections from Talks and Essays on the Spiritual Process
and God-Realization*
$7.95 paper

PRACTICAL TEXTS

EASY DEATH
*Talks and Essays on the Inherent and Ultimate
Transcendence of Death and Everything Else*
$10.95 paper

CONSCIOUS EXERCISE AND THE TRANSCENDENTAL SUN
The principle of love applied to exercise and the method of common physical action. A science of whole body wisdom, or true emotion, intended most especially for those engaged in religious or spiritual life.
$10.95 cloth, $8.95 paper

THE EATING GORILLA COMES IN PEACE
The Transcendental Principle of Life Applied to Diet and the Regenerative Discipline of True Health
$12.95 paper

RAW GORILLA
The Principles of Regenerative Raw Diet Applied in True Spiritual Practice
$3.95 paper

LOVE OF THE TWO-ARMED FORM
The Free and Regenerative Function of Sexuality in Ordinary Life, and the Transcendence of Sexuality in True Religious or Spiritual Practice
$12.95 paper

LOOK AT THE SUNLIGHT ON THE WATER
Educating Children for a Life of Self-Transcending Love and Happiness
$7.95 paper

PAMPHLETS

THE TRANSCENDENCE OF EGO AND EGOIC SOCIETY
$1.50 paper

A CALL FOR THE RADICAL REFORMATION OF CHRISTIANITY
$2.00 paper

FOR CHILDREN

WHAT TO REMEMBER TO BE HAPPY
A Spiritual Way of Life for Your First Fourteen Years or So
$3.95 paper

I AM HAPPINESS
A Rendering for Children of the Spiritual Adventure of Master Da Free John
Adapted by Daji Bodha and Lynne Closser from
The Knee of Listening *by Da Free John*
$8.95 paper

PERIODICALS

CRAZY WISDOM
The Monthly Journal of The Johannine Daist Communion
12 copies $36.00

THE LAUGHING MAN
The Alternative to Scientific Materialism and Religious Provincialism
4 copies (quarterly) $14.00

CASSETTE TAPES

UNDERSTANDING
A consideration by Da Free John
$9.95 cassette

THE FOUNDATION AND THE SOURCE
A consideration by Da Free John
$9.95 cassette

THE YOGA OF CONSIDERATION AND THE WAY THAT I TEACH
A consideration by Da Free John
$9.95 cassette

THE BODILY LOCATION OF HAPPINESS
A talk by Da Free John
$9.95 cassette

CRAZY DA MUST SING, INCLINED TO HIS
WEAKER SIDE
*Da Free John reads his Confessional Poems of Liberation
and Love*
$9.95 cassette

FEEL THE MYSTERY
*A guided meditation for children based on instructions by
Da Free John*
$7.95 cassette

DA BELLS
Tibetan "singing bowls" played by Da Free John
$8.95 cassette

HEAR MY BREATHING HEART
*Songs of Invocation and Praise Inspired by the Teaching
and Presence of Da Free John by The First Amendment
Choir*
$8.95 Dolby stereo

TRUTH IS THE ONLY PROFOUND
*Devotional readings from the Teaching of Da Free John
set to a background of devotional music and songs*
$9.95 cassette

THE TRANSCENDENCE OF FAMILIARITY
A consideration by Da Free John
$9.95 cassette

A BIRTHDAY MESSAGE FROM JESUS AND ME
A talk by Da Free John
$9.95 cassette

THE PRESUMPTION OF BEING
A consideration by Da Free John
$9.95 cassette

THE GOSPEL OF THE SIDDHAS
A talk by Da Free John
$9.95 cassette

THE COSMIC MANDALA
A talk by Da Free John
$9.95 cassette

THE ULTIMATE WISDOM OF
THE PERFECT PRACTICE
A consideration by Da Free John
$9.95 cassette

PURIFY YOURSELF WITH HAPPINESS
A consideration by Da Free John
$9.95 cassette

THE ASANA OF SCIENCE
A consideration by Da Free John
$9.95 cassette

THE HYMN OF THE MASTER
A confessional recitation of Da Free John's The Hymn
of the Master by a devotee
$7.95 cassette

VIDEOTAPES

THE BODILY LOCATION OF HAPPINESS
A consideration by Da Free John
$108, 56 minutes, VHS format

THE FIRE MUST HAVE ITS WAY
A consideration by Da Free John
$108, 57 minutes, VHS format

Classic Spiritual Literature

THE SECRET GOSPEL
The Discovery and Interpretation of the Secret Gospel
According to Mark
by Morton Smith
$7.95 paper

LONG PILGRIMAGE
The Life and Teaching of The Shivapuri Baba
by John G. Bennett
$7.95 paper

THE DIVINE MADMAN
The Sublime Life and Songs of Drukpa Kunley
translated by Keith Dowman
$7.95 paper

THE YOGA OF LIGHT
The Classic Esoteric Handbook of Kundalini Yoga
by Hans-Ulrich Rieker,
translated by Elsy Becherer
$7.95 paper

A NEW APPROACH TO BUDDHISM
by Dhiravamsa
$3.95 paper

VEDANTA AND CHRISTIAN FAITH
by Bede Griffiths
$3.95 paper

FOUNDING THE LIFE DIVINE
by Morwenna Donnelly
$7.95 paper

BREATH, SLEEP, THE HEART, AND LIFE
The Revolutionary Health Yoga of Pundit Acharya
$7.95 paper

THE SPIRITUAL INSTRUCTIONS OF
SAINT SERAPHIM OF SAROV
edited and with an introduction by Da Free John
$3.95 paper

THE SONG OF THE SELF SUPREME
Aṣṭāvakra Gītā
Preface by Da Free John
translated by Radhakamal Mukerjee
$9.95 paper

SELF-REALIZATION OF NOBLE WISDOM
The Lankavatara Sutra
compiled by Dwight Goddard on the basis of D. T.
Suzuki's rendering from the Sanskrit and Chinese
$7.95 paper

SCIENTIFIC PROOF OF THE EXISTENCE OF GOD WILL SOON BE ANNOUNCED BY THE WHITE HOUSE!

Prophetic Wisdom about the Myths and Idols of mass culture and popular religious cultism, the new priesthood of scientific and political materialism, and the secrets of Enlightenment hidden in the body of Man
DA FREE JOHN

We can all see it and feel it—though we enjoy more material prosperity, human society is decaying around us. The social and political structures of mankind seem impelled toward more and more conflict. And no increase in our scientific knowledge seems salvatory. Nor do the religious traditions of our time seem capable of bringing about significant changes. They have lost their association with the Living God. They no longer represent a creative, transforming force in the world. It is in times like ours that the need for wisdom and enlightened leadership is great.

This book by Master Da Free John is destined to serve that purpose. It is his profound and prophetic evaluation of modern mass culture, religious provincialism and fundamentalism, and the limitations of political and scientific materialism. But Master Da is more than critical. He offers us viable alternatives: the principles of true human culture, spiritual practice, and the highest Realization that is the only real peace, freedom, and happiness: the perfect transcendence of the ego and its world. We have here the voice of an Adept speaking of matters worth our mature consideration if we value the liberation which is potential in human life.

$12.95, paperback, 430 pages

EASY DEATH
Talks and Essays on the Inherent and Ultimate Transcendence of Death and Everything Else
DA FREE JOHN

"Thank you for sharing this masterpiece."

> Elisabeth Kubler-Ross, M.D.
> author, *On Death and Dying*

". . . In his writing and, I am sure, by his personal example, he is transmitting to us the greater meaning of what near-death research has only dimly seen."

> From the Foreword
> by Prof. Kenneth Ring
> author, *Life at Death*

". . . Da Free John's words about the relation of death to life, love, surrender, and transformation have a clarity of mind and emotion that feels like a fresh breeze. His words clear the atmosphere, free the energies, and make breathing easier."

> Elmer E. Green, Ph.D.
> The Menninger Foundation

Topics discussed include: what actually occurs during and after death; transcending fear; death and meditation; reincarnation; the fallacies of traditional religious beliefs about death; ego-death; how to serve the dying person; and personal experiences around death by Master Da's students.

$10.95, 400 pages. Illustrated, quality paperback

THE SECRET GOSPEL
The Discovery and Interpretation of the Secret Gospel According to Mark
BY MORTON SMITH

In 1958, Morton Smith traveled to Jerusalem to do research in the monastery library of Mar Saba, in the Judean Desert. But what he found was no routine corroboration of New Testament history, but a precious fragment of a second-century document that would change our understanding of the work and teaching of Jesus of Nazareth. Copied onto the back pages of a seventeenth-century volume was part of a letter from St. Clement of Alexandria, which makes reference to secret teachings of Jesus, apparently reserved for a special few of his disciples. The letter also quotes a passage from a "Secret Gospel" of St. Mark, telling of secret rites performed by Jesus with these disciples.

What was the Master imparting on these occasions that was not part of his public ministry? Why are there so many traces of it in the New Testament? And why was it kept hidden?

As exciting as the most suspenseful adventure story, Professor Smith's book is a lively and readable account of the discovery and unraveling of some of Christianity's most intriguing mysteries.

$7.95 paperback, 157 pages

This is a brilliant account of how Morton Smith reached a major discovery in the study of first-century Christianity. We have not only his conclusions and the way in which these are argued, but also his own life and thought as he reached them. The discovery itself ranks with Qumran and Nag Hammadi, Masada and the Cairo Geniza, but required more learning and sheer erudition than all of these together, both in the recognition of what had been found, and in the interpretation and explanation of the meaning of the find. All this Smith has done—and he tells us about it in a narrative of exceptional charm and simplicity.

Jacob Neusner, Professor of
Religious Studies
Brown University

THE DREADED GOM-BOO, OR THE IMAGINARY DISEASE THAT RELIGION SEEKS TO CURE
A Collection of Essays and Talks on the "Direct" Process of Enlightenment
DA FREE JOHN

In this book Master Da presents a startling and humorous insight—all religion seeks to cure us of an unreal disease, which he calls the "Dreaded Gom-boo." This disease is our constant assumption that we have fallen from Grace and are thus in need of religious belief as a salvatory "cure."

Master Da uproots this religious conceit and illusion by confessing that we are always, already present and alive as Divine Being. The "good news" of his Way is that we need not seek to be cured but must only feel, observe, understand, and renounce the very activity of seeking itself, and thus be restored to our native Happiness and Freedom. The liberating message of this book cuts through thousands of years of religious and mystical dogma and beliefs by revealing a radical spiritual Way eminently suited to the needs of modern Westerners.

$9.95, 400 pages, quality paperback

CASSETTES

THE PRESUMPTION OF BEING

A consideration by Da Free John

In this talk containing excerpts from "Tell Me True—Have You Got the Gom-Boo?" published in Master Da Free John's book *The Dreaded Gom-Boo, or the Imaginary Disease That Religion Seeks to Cure,* Master Da humorously argues that a fundamental doubt of Being is the "dreaded disease" of egoity for which all people seek a cure. Master Da then describes the true spiritual process wherein we presently transcend all sense of dis-ease and pursuit of cure and magnify our intuitive feeling of Happiness and the native presumption of Being.

$9.95, cassette tape

THE GOSPEL OF THE SIDDHAS

A talk by Da Free John

In this historic talk from 1973, Master Da Free John gives his first full explanation of the Divine process of his function as Spiritual Master for devotees. In response to questions from his students, Master Da describes the true spiritual practice of "Satsang," or spiritual intimacy with a true Spiritual Master, as the Way of living Truth and not a means to or search for Truth. The full text of this talk appears in Master Da's book, *The Method of the Siddhas.*

$9.95, cassette tape

A BIRTHDAY MESSAGE FROM JESUS AND ME

A talk by Da Free John

This recorded talk by Master Da Free John contains selections from his commentary on the essay entitled, "A Birthday Message from Jesus and Me," published in *The Fire Gospel: Essays and Talks on Spiritual Baptism.* In this talk, given on his birthday, November 3, 1982, Master Da proclaims that the essential root of true religion is Spirit Baptism, or entrance into Communion with the Living Spirit-Being, which is God, Truth, Reality, and Happiness. Master Da also identifies this Spirit-religion with the fundamental Teaching of Jesus and contrasts it with the myth-based religion of conventional Christianity.

$9.95, cassette tape

THE TRANSCENDENCE OF FAMILIARITY

A consideration by Da Free John

In this talk Master Da argues that our common presumption of familiarity with all things, even our selves, is only a presumption and that in Truth we exist in a state of Ignorance. We do not know what anything is. In this restatement of one of the principal Arguments of his Teaching, Master Da draws devotees into the consideration that true understanding, or Enlightenment, lies in the capacity to stand as free awareness of the mere "Isness" of all conditions via the "transcendence of familiarity."

$9.95, cassette tape

THE LAUGHING MAN
MAGAZINE

Twentieth-century advances in communications and transportation now make the world's philosophies, religions, and spiritual paths equally accessible to all. But universal communication has thus far led us further into chaos, rather than to understanding. The influence of scientific materialism and religious provincialism has scattered and divided mankind by substituting partial truths for the Whole.

THE LAUGHING MAN is dedicated to bringing the light of Radical Understanding to this confusing situation. The magazine's unique format, based on the description of the seven stages of life as developed by Master Da Free John, provides a lively forum for the critical consideration of traditional wisdom as well as contemporary issues and concerns.

Join us as we enter into free dialogue with the many traditions and viewpoints. Take advantage of this opportunity to become acquainted with the clarifying Teaching of Master Da Free John, and to be inspired by accounts of his Transforming Work with devotees. Simply fill out the subscription form and mail it today. We look forward to serving you.

Free sample copy with any books ordered from these pages (see order form).

ORDER FORM

THE DAWN HORSE PRESS
Dept. GE, P.O. Box 3680, Clearlake, CA 95422

BOOKS

☐ The Dreaded Gom-Boo, or the Imaginary Disease
That Religion Seeks to Cure .... Da Free John $9.95
☐ Long Pilgrimage .... John G. Bennett $7.95
☐ Scientific Proof of the Existence of God Will Soon
Be Announced by the White House! .... Da Free John $12.95
☐ The Secret Gospel .... Morton Smith $7.95
☐ Easy Death .... Da Free John $10.95

_____   _____

_____   _____

_____   _____

_____   _____

_____   _____

TAPES

☐ The Transcendence of Familiarity $9.95
☐ A Birthday Message from Jesus and Me $9.95
☐ The Presumption of Being $9.95
☐ The Gospel of the Siddhas $9.95

☐ Yes, send me a copy of Laughing Man magazine with my order.

Subtotal _____

California residents add 6% sales tax _____

Please add $1.25 postage and handling for first
item and $.35 for each additional item _____

TOTAL AMOUNT _____

☐ Enclosed is my check or money order
made payable to The Dawn Horse Press.
☐ I wish to use my ☐ VISA ☐ MASTERCARD

Card No. _____

Expiration Date _____

Signature _____

Name _____

Address _____

City _____ State _____ Zip _____